FITTING IN

FITTING IN
Crosswise
at
Generation
Gap

HERBERT LONDON

Grosset & Dunlap
PUBLISHERS
NEW YORK

Grateful acknowledgment is made to the editors of *New York* magazine in which part of this book originally appeared. "Underground Notes from a Campus Ombudsman," by Herbert London, is reprinted from the *Journal of Higher Education*, 41 (May, 1970), pp. 350–64. Copyright © 1970 by the Ohio State University Press. All rights reserved.

To Mom and Dad, and to Stacy and Nancy—all of whom contributed to this book in more ways than they know

Contents

Preface

THERE I WAS, sitting in a supposedly chic East Side place called Le Drugstore, eating a hamburger that costs $2.75. The people around me were like a species I had not seen before. If I closed my eyes and reopened them quickly, I could see a circus of hair, colors, and frantic gestures. I always thought of myself as reasonably hip; I was the "best-dressed boy" in my high school graduating class. But this scene made me feel peculiar. What the hell was I doing eating a hamburger that costs $2.75 among people who were as strange as any I've seen?

I could have left. But I kept asking myself if I looked as strange to them as they did to me. And the more I thought about it, the more I realized I was different. I was somewhat older, more conservative in dress and appearance, and, after overhearing a conversation, light-years away from that social scene.

Several weeks later, I found myself in a setting that was

equally perplexing. I was drinking a beer at a bar on Sixth Avenue and Twelfth Street. Nothing pretentious, mind you: oilcloth table coverings, spaceship decals on the wall, and a sea of dirty white T-shirts at the bar. Hamburgers cost fifty-five cents and the jukebox selections were restricted to Johnny Cash. I didn't experience the same sense of incongruity that prevailed in Le Drugstore, but I was uneasy, and I certainly didn't belong.

For several years now I've been trying to describe this contrast and my own peculiar reaction to it. At the outset I was analytical, as college professors are supposed to be. I wrote about the changing social scene, the alteration in values and political polarization, in many cases before it became hackneyed to do so. My work was published in scholarly journals and, in a couple of instances, even received some recognition. One copy of a 1969 journal in which I published an article does not even have dust on the cover despite the fact that it lies in an obscure corner of the New York University library. What greater recognition can an academic receive?

Nonetheless, I think I am ready for something else. It's not that I despair over research. On the contrary, I feel it is time to write about something I've seen and lived, not read. For once I want to write without getting dusty in the old stack room. Lest this be interpreted as an unwitting academic cop-out, let me note that it is done quite knowingly. This is my gut history of the fifties and sixties, a history filled with personal events that link my life to a generation.

FITTING IN

CHAPTER 1
Between Two Cultures

I AM A PRODUCT OF I.C.—intergenerational confusion—a curious psychological state afflicting those who identify with neither Consciousness III nor the Organization Man. Intergenerational confusion is a manifestation of having been born after the Depression but before the baby boom. It usually means, in effect, that one is too old to "Do It!" yet too young not to try. I.C. is not something I discovered. The symptoms are quite apparent to any atavistic Nixon hater who, at the same time, found the McGovern candidacy abhorrent. Would you believe that products of I.C. preferred Hubie? Not the Humphrey of L.B.J., but the one who supported the civil rights plank in the Democratic party platform of 1948, the one who initiated the nuclear test ban and replaced F.D.R. as an American idol (in Jewish homes).

Yet I.C. is by no means just a political expression. It is an ideological chasm for contemporary social misfits; it is the place for unapologetic rock freaks who envisioned Wood-

Bacchanalia; it is a refuge for those whose hair is longer
than Senator James Buckley's but are unwilling to adopt the
Frank Zappa look; it is a rejection of the country club and
the East Side orgy; it is a reluctance to embrace "radical
chic" or conservative WASP snobbery; it is being turned off
by both the bluing and the greening of America; it is also a
sneering at both *The New York Review* and *The National
Review*. In short, I.C. is stylistic bewilderment.

It wasn't always this way. At the time of white bucks,
V-neck sweaters, tan trousers, and crew cuts, I knew exactly
where I stood. I was a Stevensonian Democrat with idealistic
views about civil rights, an inherited admiration for Norman Thomas, a love of sports that bordered on obsession,
and an insatiable hunger for pictures of Natalie Wood. I
went to films as often as I could, studied only out of a com-
pulsion to succeed, was shy with girls, knew every statistic in
the baseball record book, believed that competition is the
midwife of excellence, and let John make my shelf so I
could pass shop in return for one week's math homework.
(Needless to say, I got the better of that deal.) I was a
classic fifties type who had New York schoolyard dust and
New York Post print all over him. George Orwell, Jackie
Robinson, and Holden Caulfield were my heroes. I read *A
Stone for Danny Fisher* as soon as my parents left the house
and called a lovely redhead who sat next to me in class
only to choke up when I tried to ask her out. I could sit for
hours throwing a ball against a wall and fantasizing about a
game-winning catch I would make in the World Series. I
would hang out in front of the bowling alley half listening
to a conversation about girls while I hummed "Why Do
Fools Fall in Love?" The world wasn't a better place, but it
was certainly simpler. There were still a few standards one

2

could count on. For example, a party was really a party—
kids danced since they didn't know about turning on; parents *let* you use the car—no one under eighteen had inalien-
able rights; a teacher might be abused but you usually knew
when to draw the line—a tear in her eye was enough to
make you apologetic; and guys were measured by their ability to stuff a basketball or hit three sewers. We didn't
believe God was in His heaven, and we certainly didn't
believe all was right with the world; but we did not yet
have an identity crisis—if anyone spoke of alienation, he
would have been referred to Casa Mama's for a pizza and
coke, the teen-age cure-all.

Sure, times have changed; Bob Dylan reminded me of that
all through the sixties. Yet I am in no small part a product
of my experiences; I view the world through a fifties prism.
It's not rose-colored, but it certainly isn't gray either. Having been suckled on virulent anti-McCarthyism, I view orthodoxies with suspicion, be they of the Marcusean or Birch
variety. I am a product of a relativism that too often argued
"on the one hand, yet on the other." Still, I learned and
retained a respect for the complexity of social problems. I
studied under C. Wright Mills at Columbia, yet became
critical of his theory of the "power elite" as a functional
description of American leadership. I always thought that
conspiracy theories were part of an academic's flotsam and
jetsam. By the time I reached adulthood every behavioral
principle I had learned had been called into question. For
me, the sixties were an Orwellian nightmare, a Woody Allen
stream of consciousness. Achievement was decadence;
thoughtfulness was fence-sitting; concern was bourgeois
sentimentality; liberalism was fascism. I started the decade
by embracing the New Left and ended it by giving the finger
to Tom Hayden. In the fifties Kirkpatrick and other mem-

bers of the right-wing press would have been palpably absurd to me; now, despite my basic instincts, they sometimes make sense—on some issues, such as the monopoly of the press, they are C. Wright Mills all over again.

My students tell me the times have passed me by. Perhaps they have, although students are notoriously poor judges of their own times. Perhaps I am being conservatized by age and responsibility—a phenomenon often described by American social critics. Even so iconoclastic a critic of American culture as Randolph Bourne could write, "If you are not an idealist by the time you're twenty, you don't have a heart, but if you are still an idealist by thirty, you don't have a head." But is it that simple? If my attitudes are solely a function of aging, why do I feel so uneasy? Why do I embrace so much that is contemporary? What is the explanation behind my equivocation?

My college contemporaries—once seduced by corporate recruiters and now protected by picket fences and roller skates at the front door—remain an enigma to me. I don't really speak to them, as much as I sometimes want to, yet I'm also not a very good listener in their presence. I should —or at least I think I should—know about stock options and tax shelters, but I can't generate enough interest to find out. I am generally not condescending, yet that is the way I am often described by these so-called friends. They are not cardboard Tom Raths searching for security. They are bright, earnest people eager for wealth and the comforts that money can provide. But despite my sharing a desire for wealth with them, we don't hit it off. There is a distance between us born of different generational views. They are relaxed fifties products, content in the knowledge that their values bring demonstrable rewards. I am an inveterate soul

4

mate of I.C.; as much as both of us may want it, the two styles don't mix well.

Similarly, the flower children and the progeny of Aquarius also turn me off. Their simplistic descriptions of their own lives are the litany of innocence, except that innocence has now been rediscovered as the millennium. Truth, Beauty, Goodness, Peace, Love: the catechism rolls off the tongue the way I memorized and said my Bar Mitzvah speech. Sure, the values are fine, but everyone from General Curtis Le May to Joan Baez wants peace. Is it merely enough to imbibe the spirit? Do we enter the new age by willing it? As a product of the hard-work, extreme-effort, nothing-comes-easy school, I swallow instant gratification as easily as chicken bones.

In an effort to identify with the adversary culture, I devoured every "new culture" book off the presses as quickly as John Leonard. But invariably they were disappointments. The best of these sources, William Irwin Thompson's *At the Edge of History*, left me with an unrestrained scowl. Thompson, sheltered by uptight upper middle class proprieties, thinks he has found the symptoms of a transformed culture at an integrated nude bathing scene at Esalen. All I could recall after reading that passage was skinny-dipping with Verna Lerner (I'll never forget that name) at Brighton Beach in the sixth grade. Sure, it was euphoric; sure, Brighton Beach is not Big Sur. But if skinny-dipping is the sign of a new culture, kissing a girl must be a magical rite. What Thompson reveals is his insulation. From his description of Watts it is apparent that he conceives of every black as a potential Malcolm X. It is equally apparent that he never spoke to a black before he was eighteen. For someone from the lower middle class who didn't discover his class consciousness until he was middle-aged, I always found blacks,

5

especially those who lived next door, to be like everyone else, except that they accepted welfare checks more readily and had kids who were somewhat less disciplined. But to suggest that Betty Smith or her son Roger, my friend, was transforming the culture would have led to uncontrolled laughter among the ubiquitous summer street sitters on Neptune Avenue who were searching for a breath of cool air.

But if this analysis of Thompson appears harsh, it is a mere trifle compared to my wrath for Charles Reich. In Reich's utopia the heroes wear jeans, share a communal bedroom, and groove on Elton John. Yet those with I.C. remember that scene very well indeed. I wore jeans, not as a protest, admittedly, but because my folks couldn't afford anything else. I shared a bedroom with my parents until I was twelve, and, Charles Reich notwithstanding, it wasn't pleasant. And even though Elton John wasn't around, I had James Brown's "Midnight Special" playing every minute of the day; and I could imitate every inflection in Presley's rendition of "Heartbreak Hotel." I lived vicariously through Presley, but isn't that what really happens to contemporary rock freaks? By separating American life into three levels of consciousness, Reich avoids the interstices—the products of I.C. Every designation is a crude stereotype. Do we, the members of I.C., have any role in this society? Is there no idiosyncratic culture? Must we choose between Con II and Con III? If Reich, like Cleaver, is asking whether I'm part of the problem or part of the solution, the answer is an unequivocal "neither."

If Reich acts out his neurosis through beads, "the dry look," bell bottoms, and *I Ching*, John Aldridge's *In the Country of the Young* displays a malice toward youth culture approaching unmitigated hate. True, the guitar strains are often simple and unimaginative, the faces sometimes

6

vapid, the feet dirty, and the language strained, but is his entire generalization valid? Is Iowa becoming the East Village? Is the youth cult inexorable? Is the "now" sound really more monotonous than Frank Sinatra? Aldridge identifies himself as a child of the Depression, the other side of the universe from Con III. He is just unable to appreciate any value in rock, and he is equally myopic about refinements gone astray. He is a literary WASP who has made no compromises with postwar America. Without him there is no dialectic; he is the different culture against which adversary culture reacts. He represents the measuring rod of the past. But he is as alien to those members of I.C. as he is to admirers of the Rolling Stones. Obviously, the literature of the so-called "new culture" has no answers for me.

Still, there are hopeful signs, isolated elements of the youth movement I can salute. *Sergeant Pepper* was a brilliant album, an experiment in musical sound that could not have been attempted by even a Chuck Berry. "Good Vibrations," a tune by the Beach Boys, is a harmonically perfect fugue with a rhythmic beat. The rediscovery of Bogart and Cagney indicates that youthful film tastes haven't been totally corrupted by too large a dose of Mike Nichols. Woody Allen is a genius when it comes to recognizing neuroses in himself that are universally shared. Mailer is a sometimes more serious Allen, but he is always incisive. Revisionist historians have added a new dimension to historical analysis by stressing the social instead of the exclusively political narrative. And there are undoubtedly other contributions. A listing of the achievements of the youth movement reveals more than just accomplishments, however; it also discloses a glaring lack of discrimination. For the youth cult there is too often no distinction between Bergman and Nichols, the Beatles and Sha-Na-Na, Herbert Marcuse

7

and Angela Davis, *Playboy* and *Screw*, Carl Oglesby and Abbie Hoffman, grass and smack, highs and lows.

Egalitarianism has gone wild. To discriminate makes you an elitist. Yet for those marked by I.C., not to discriminate makes you a boor. If everyone has something to contribute, no one can be ignored. For an I.C. type like myself, the dilemma of the sixties can be traced to the fact that Americans were allowed to entertain a conception of themselves that could not be satisfied by egalitarian solutions. Narcissism is not thwarted by altruism. The sixties was a mass ego trip both for those individuals who saw paths leading to money and glory as well as for those who could just afford to be different and appear on the Johnny Carson show. With taste being abandoned, novelty was enough to ensure success —that and good publicity. McLuhan may be the charlatan of the age, but he is right in suggesting that something seen often enough will be remembered. A disc jockey once told me the same thing: "Son," he said, "there is no such thing as a good record. If I play it—play it often—it's a hit." Since I was raised on a pabulum called merit, those words still ring in my ears. Let your hair grow; let your voice rise; do something bizarre. Making it means doing all those things that only a decade ago would have spelled failure. And where does that leave the I.C. people? Too young to have invaded the boardroom of AT&T and too old to disrobe in public parks, we remain passive observers, alternately amused and mortified.

A friend once told me what may be an apocryphal story on the subject of how to get ahead, seventies style. It is the kind of tale that simultaneously enrages and perplexes those of us in I.C. A young man who had grown up in a family possessed of average means had achieved average grades and now sought a scholarship from an above-average university. Since there was nothing distinctive about the youth, his request for aid was denied, as was his application for admission. Three months later, he was arrested for armed robbery, found guilty, and sent to prison. While serving his term in jail he learned of a scholarship program for inmates sponsored by the university that had previously denied his application. This time he applied, was accepted, and was granted a full scholarship. The moral of the story is: chutzpah has its own built-in reward. Yet products of I.C. were taught "if you have it, *don't* flaunt it," a lesson that now puts us at a distinct disadvantage.

This, of course, is not the only disadvantage we face. I.C. types are equally awkward at parties where everyone turns on or at country clubs where handicaps and Johnnie Walker are discussed. We sit uneasily through porno films, and find Doris Day boring as hell. The hip view us as hopelessly square, and the white-haired Darien dudes see us as hopelessly uninformed. We don't make the Ivy League because "mau-mauing the flak catchers" was not one of our operational lessons, yet we are not poor enough to be subsidized by a public institution. We dare not travel in parts of the South for fear that our lengthening sideburns will be treated with suspicion, and we are rejected at Max's Kansas City for hair that doesn't cover the ear.

Yet even if it is rejection that sets me apart, I have learned one important lesson from all this: I'm proud of what I am. (Perhaps it would be more appropriate to say that I am proud of what I am not.) I.C. types do have an ethos. It is not formally expressed, but it can be recognized by members of the clan. While strolling through Washington Square Park one day, I couldn't help but notice this well-endowed babe cross my path with bouncing breasts that were threatening to elude her halter. Since her appearance was obviously designed to attract attention, I stared; so did a man at my right. For an instant our eyes met, and I saw a look that immediately signaled I.C. This fellow, intrigued by the woman, didn't know what to make of her, and the wry smile on his lips suggested that he was equally aware of my befuddled response. We were clansmen meeting by chance in a situation only I.C. types could appreciate.

On a dimly lit subway car a man who was apparently blind asked me for money. Being a Manhattanite for almost ten years, I ritualistically dropped a dime in his tin cup. This scene was observed by several people in the car. Two stops later I left the train with the blind man walking in front of me. I noticed that he ducked behind a stairwell, removed his dark glasses, and proceeded up the steps without assistance. Just as I realized I had been taken, one observer of my charitable gesture raised a hand that denoted half-hearted resignation. The gesture could not have been made by anyone other than an I.C. type. An older man would have displayed a fist; a younger man would have smiled approvingly, admiringly. But *that* gesture was a genuine I.C. expression, and for an instant it was nice to know someone else knew exactly how I felt.

A common spirit unites I.C. types. But no major social critic has identified the I.C. cultural phenomenon. We have not been discovered by Susan Sontag. In fact, it is our very exclusion that sets us apart. But at times, I admit, it would be comforting to have a sign, an overt symbol, to hold us together instead of the subtle gestures and wry smiles from which we must intuit camaraderie. If the young can preempt the victory sign; if the blue-collar worker can make hardhats de rigueur; if Madison Avenue can insist on high-vented jackets, why can't the I.C. generation find a symbol? Perhaps the answer is to have the initials I.C. tattooed on one's wrist.

No, the cycle gangs have pretty well captured the tattoo market. Perhaps the answer is a Paul Stuart blazer with an I.C. crest on the chest pocket. Unfortunately, yachters have crests locked up this year. There is, of course, that resigned hand gesture, but any hand in the air is likely to be identified with Stokely Carmichael or Bella Abzug—very bad associations for I.C. people. The answer is simple: no symbol at all. In an age of omnipresent symbols—from cults, clothes, handshakes, and buttons to slogans, clubs, insignias, and flags—what better way to unify a new group than to do nothing that sets you apart? I.C. comrades can unite by not joining anyone (or anything) else. By a process of elimination we do have a sign: our simplicity.

The reader, at this point, especially the one who does not identify with I.C., is probably asking himself, why all the fuss? But if you have to ask this question, there is no sense in reading further. This is not an exercise in self-indulgence. My life does have idiosyncratic features, but I am clearly a product of I.C. No, it's not my age (thirty-four), nor my class (combatively lower-middle), nor the imprint of the fifties, although each of these factors, in turn, contributed to my I.C. condition. There are, after all, aging "radical chic" types desperately trying to retain their youth through identification with Con III artifacts purchased at Azuma or Bloomingdale's. There are lower-middle-class individuals who compensate for their past by means of affected British accents, Gucci pocketbooks, and sneering indictments of the ethnics. (Why, do you realize those ethnics live in *attached* houses?) And there are former Brooklyn Dodger fans, crew cuts, and even Eisenhower supporters who now have hair curling down their necks, flaunt unwieldy beards, and roll their own joints. Obviously, many individuals possessing a background similar to mine acquiesced to contemporary

11

social forces. In most cases they chose to be fashionable, which meant the East Side co-op, dinner at Maxwell's Plum, key parties, and knowing smiles at unintelligible lines from a Godard film. There are some who took another path of little resistance and joined the adversaries of the adversary culture. Here are the "Joes," the red-white-and-blue parades, and the love-it-or-leave-it tough talk. It's pizza on Friday night, women should know their place, "I'll give you the back of my hand" logic, and "why don't they make movies like they used to?" Needless to say, I am not in either of these groups. I remain firm in my conviction that it is between these cultures that I belong. It is not recognition that I want, albeit I.C. has been ignored far too long; it is my simple desire to make the voice of my generation heard amidst all the other noise.

CHAPTER 2
An Early Rock
Freak Wails

ASIDE FROM SPORTS, rock music had the most profound influence on my social development as a youth. I would stay up half the night listening to WINS. Without really trying, I memorized every lyric in the Top Fifty for every year from 1956 to 1959. There wasn't a trick in Presley's lyrical repertoire that I couldn't imitate and, if I may indulge my fantasies, do even better than Elvis. And he had an echo chamber; all I had was my shower. Most of my few friends never shared my enthusiasm for rock. It lacked sophistication, so they said. Belafonte, on the other hand, turned them on; but after two listenings to "Hold 'Em Joe," I couldn't wait to retreat into my private world of Alan Freed and Moondog. From my point of view, you had to be in a teen-age executive training program to think Belafonte could compare with the Coasters.

I can't be sure now that rock lyrics ever had any meaning for me. James Baldwin notwithstanding, I never could discover black rage in the indecipherable "shu be dus" of "Get A Job," just as I didn't know, till years later, that "C. C. Rider" had a very special meaning for junkies. What I found in rock music was a style that combined rebellious verve with a conventional message. I was "Johnny B. Goode" and "Charlie Brown." Though I didn't know it at the time, rock was one of my earliest exposures to I.C. Presley and Berry offended with their style, not their words. They were as dedicated to getting ahead—big cars, love, and church bells—as was Norman Vincent Peale, but few ever listened to their message; they just saw it. And what they saw was a blatant assault on morality through pelvic gyrations and the caressing of a phallic guitar. Early rock style appears almost Victorian by contemporary standards, but in its time it was a vicarious sexual experience for eager but naive teenagers.

By the time I could drive a car, the dial was set to New York's preeminent rock station, and the music was turned up loud enough to attract every girl parading on Union Turnpike. Rock associations were all positive for me: the driving rhythmic beat, high-pitched squeals, and hair blowing in the breeze. I even went to "stroll" parties and devised variations for this dance that had not yet been discovered on the Dick Clark show. Rock was undiluted pleasure. It gave you the nerve to dance without going to a Fred Astaire studio first. It was always a conversation piece. ("Do you know who recorded 'Earth Angel' first?") And it let you be a part of a group without synthetic social chatter. All you had to do was hum, beat the chair, or let your knees shake. The music was functional; what my parents' generation never realized was that early rock made awkward teen-agers feel a little less self-conscious. Ironically, post-Dylan music, primarily designed for listening, has reintroduced that original sense of awkwardness; this, to some extent, helps explain the youthful "eagerness" to turn on. It's not only that Dylan's progeny are more sophisticated, as some social critics allege, but that they simply don't know what else to do at a party.

Since my mom was one of those crazies who waited two hours at the Paramount to see Perry Como and Frank Sinatra, it was only natural that I should have a similar fascination with pop music. Show business, from vaudeville to film and pop music, was always considered something special in our house. My mom did have an early singing career that included several radio spots and my dad insists that he was being groomed as a cantor for his Bayonne, New Jersey, synagogue. To this day I'm convinced that, had "The $64,000 Question" been legit, my mom could have cleaned up. She can still tell you how many Hollywood starlets are divorced, and she reads *Photoplay* the way I devoured baseball record books. She was the original film freak. When I was a kid—and even later—she would put some meat in a pot, turn the burners down, and drag me to the local movie house—a place called "The Dumps." If it was a Joan Crawford–Lana Turner double-feature, we'd stay for three showings. My dad could usually tell how good the film was by what he had for dinner: a thick soup was a one-star film, stew meant two stars, and a charred roast was a four-star special.

By the time I was four, I had memorized half the dialogue in *Public Enemy Number One*. In fact, I spent my time daydreaming about what was likely to happen at the *Perils of Pauline* serial I would see on Saturday. By the time I was seven, I could floor any crowd with my rendition of any Al Jolson tune. With a little parental coaching and coaxing, I would get up at a family gathering to do my "Mammy" or "April Showers" routine. For me, the only social contacts I ever really had were on the stage. Being in front of an audience was a magic elixir; I could do things I never dreamed were possible. Off stage, however, I was as inaudible and quiet as the original Mumbles. I lived a considerable portion of my youth not as Herb London but as Al Jolson, Nat King Cole, Elvis Presley, Gene Vincent, and Bobby Darin.

By the time I reached high school, I could really wail. And it was no wonder, for I certainly practiced enough. I once sang the complete version of "Sha Boom" 128 times in succession. On one rainy weekend I did nothing but listen to Roy Hamilton's record of "Ebb Tide"—until I thought I would drown in that rushing tide. I bought every issue of *Song Hits* and eagerly sought out errors in the printed lyrics. Yet at school my musical talent remained undisclosed, and for a very good reason.

In music class I was happy to wail "Go Down Moses" at the top of my well-developed lungs. My teacher, who was also coach of the choir, wanted to discover the source of that resonant voice. Had I revealed my other self (something I wanted to do), I would have been in her choir, but that would have meant having to miss basketball practice. And if there was one thing more important than singing, it was basketball. So when she stared inquisitively into my eyes and said, "Sing," I tried desperately to give her my Stanley Einbender impersonation. (Stanley was a close friend who had a singing voice like Jackie Leonard's.) To no one's surprise, it worked. I resolved my first major psychological conflict with honors.

But even though I didn't sing in school, my interest in rock remained undiminished. Without realizing it, I not only had learned the lyrics to every popular hit (and many an obscure tune), but I could also name every label and each company's "stable" of stars. Knowing rock trivia was almost as important to me as knowing how many times Ty Cobb led the American League in batting. And, despite what you may think, this information paid off. Since I had all the social graces of King Kong with girls, I could sometimes conceal my awkwardness by telling them on what label Screaming Jay Hawkins recorded. It was undoubtedly better than telling them that George Kell beat Ted Williams by two tenths of a percentage point to win the American League batting crown in 1949. With most of the girls I knew, I could usually be counted on for my record information bit. It certainly wasn't what you'd call romantic, but it was either that or George Kell's batting feats.

It wasn't until I started going to summer camp that my stage presence truly emerged. I had never realized what a summer camp was all about. When I was of camp age, summers were spent at a Coney Island beach, which I usually reached by surreptitiously hopping aboard a trolley car. With the unspent nickel (for carfare) my mom gave me, I could get a Nathan's Famous hot dog on the way home. That was the way to spend a summer; camps were for fags, or so I thought. One year my folks did send me to a Boy Scout camp for two weeks; they probably felt guilty about my never having been to the country. It was there that I discovered just how backward I really was. In two days I almost cut off my toe with an ax; spent two sleepless nights trying to repair a hole in my tent, which on dry nights was a kamikaze run for mosquitoes and on wet nights was a miniature Victoria Falls; got second-degree burns on two fingers when I tried to make a fire; and returned home emaciated because I wouldn't eat raw potatoes. Boy Scout camp was an eye-opening experience. But that is not the kind of summer camp to which I'm referring.

By the time I was a high school junior and something of

17

an accomplished basketball player, my coach asked me if I
would be a junior counselor at his camp. This was not a
build-yourself-a-tent setup; it was an upper-middle-class
camp with roomy cabins, indoor toilets, and hot-and-cold
running water. Since everyone else there bitched about the
crude conditions, I was reluctant to say they were a damned
sight better than any I had seen before. But there was no
sense in wearing my class origins like a chip on the shoulder.
I was there to play basketball; and Coach had brought me
up to the camp to develop my skills, not coincidentally, to
be a cheap source of labor. (It was a "free summer," he
said. I later learned exactly what that meant: I got room and
board and he got free labor.)

As things turned out, I did more than play basketball.
Since the camp was self-conscious about its emphasis on
sports, it had "cultural events" as part of a color war epic.
These events were a sop to parents to make them believe that
the camp was forming well-rounded youngsters. (Since the
usual eating fare consisted of every known variety of pasta,
that belief was not entirely wrong.) At group sings I revealed an aspect of myself that had been carefully guarded.
For Coach I was little more than a stud with an uncanny soft
touch at twenty-five feet. But at sings I made sexy incanta-
tions like Nat Cole and Presley. I even went so far as to get a
blond wig and guitar for effect. When I did my "Heartbreak
Hotel," the old wooden dining hall reverberated with
screams. For twelve-year-old "senior" campers I was an
instant heartthrob. Even Coach had to admit that I made the
summer for half the girls' camp. I've referred to this effect
as the pre-adolescent Marjorie Morningstar syndrome. It
was especially pronounced at co-ed camps where the girls
were under twelve and the assistant counselors fifteen. I
could be big brother, Ricky Nelson, and sweet dreams all

rolled into one, with no complications. For this audience I usually did my Cole rendition of "They Tried to Tell Us We're Too Young" or "Too Young to Go Steady." These tunes hit romantic nerve endings like an astringent on a muggy day.

It was at one of these sings, three summers later, that I was "discovered." An enterprising counselor several years my senior said, "You should be recording. With those looks and that voice you'll drive 'em crazy." From that moment on I thought of myself as a pro. I had visions of traveling around the world to critical acclaim, beautiful women dangling from each arm, and a custom Rolls Royce at my doorstep bearing the inscription "Herbi." (The fifties, for those in the know, was the "i" generation.) With just a few compliments and some very tentative arrangements, the Walter Mitty in me took over. I started to daydream about the future, and the dreams proved not entirely false.

The counselor in whom I had placed my faith had more enterprising zeal than I had imagined. Within a few months of the end of camp, he had set up an audition, provisions for a demonstration record, and a very handsome contract for himself. A little too much vigor always made me uneasy, but the Walter Mitty in me kept saying, "Cool it, you're on the way, baby." The record company proved to be somewhat less reputable than R.C.A., but it *was* a record company, and from my knowledge of recording history it was apparent that one or two hits made a label. I was being plugged as a future rock star by a firm called Buzz. Bright lights were continually blinking in front of me. I ate lunch at Lindy's and chatted with company executives at an office immediately above the Irving Berlin Music Co.

My manager, heretofore my counselor friend, never stopped talking about the way to cash in. But at that point we had done nothing but spend money on "promos" (I was even starting to talk like a show biz type) and some professional pictures. The great day finally came when my manager (he was becoming more of a manager and less of a friend) said, "I've lined up two guys in Philly who write for Fabian and Avalon. It's a can't-miss arrangement." This guy was now running faster than Sammy Glick, and his talk outstripped his movement. We went to Philadelphia, where, for two solid days, these guys wrote lyrics that would have embarrassed "bubble gum" fiends in the sixties, and I, between swigs of Cheracol, sang them. I wasn't pleased with the results, but after that trial by ordeal I would have been happy to record "Hickory Dickory Dock." The songs were entitled "We're Not Going Steady" and "Hey Red!"—not exactly sententious, but they did evoke Nat King Cole and Elvis associations, or so I thought. Then, when I had two songs and the hard job seemed over, I learned that the real work was only beginning.

Two executives from Buzz introduced me to Bobby Smith, a company A&R (arranging and recording) man who had worked with some of "the most renown people" in the business, I was told. It was always hard for me to distinguish between the superlatives in biz-people conversation, so I couldn't be sure of just how "renown" his former clients had been. One thing, however, was revealing: we didn't eat at Lindy's across the street, but at the Bickford's on the corner. Yet Bobby turned out to be the most genuine person I met in my short-lived rock career. He was pure soul, even before the notion became fashionable. He arranged songs for Mahalia Jackson, Roy Hamilton, and Sam "The Man" Taylor, and it had all rubbed off. He did, indeed, know the luminaries.

After Bobby had heard me sing for the first time, he

called me "a white Roy Hamilton." He took me to Hamilton recording sessions, and, as I had done so many times before, I started to make indelible mental notes of his style. In no time at all I managed to live up to the name tag I was given. All those hours of listening to "Ebb Tide" appeared to be related to some transcendent force I called fate. Since I cannot read music, Bobby "interpreted" my two "handpicked" songs for me. And despite my initial disinclination, "We're Not Going Steady" took on a distinct soul quality that was totally inconsistent with the lyrics, yet gave the piece an appealing quality. Can you imagine Frankie Avalon recording for early Motown?

Every day, immediately after lunch, Bobby would meet me at my fraternity house, and we would jam at an old piano that had cranked out college songs for too long. "Steady," which is the way Bobby referred to our record, "was comin', yeah, it's comin'." That was all I had to hear: the "white Roy Hamilton" was on his way.

Finally, after three months of daily practice at that untuned piano, he said, "You're ready; in one week we record." I was so damn nervous, I didn't sleep for two straight nights. I had had experience in front of an audience, but this was different. All I could think of was that recording session and what I believed was at stake.

The night before recording was to begin, I stood in front of the mirror acting out all my Elvis motions. Then I took every stitch of clothing from my wardrobe, dumped it on my bed, and rummaged through the pile until I discovered exactly the right combination—a blazer, a pair of white jeans, and a sport shirt unbuttoned to reveal the sprouting hairs on my chest. It seems bizarre now, but when I walked into the recording studio no one even noticed me, a fact I attributed to my appropriate selection of clothes. In retrospect, no one would have noticed me if I had appeared bare-assed. Bobby gave me a stay-loose sign, but there was no way I could relax. When I saw the musicians, my kneecaps quivered so hard I thought they would walk away on their own. There was Mickey of Mickey & Sylvia fame on guitar, a drummer, a bass player I had seen at Brooklyn Paramount rock shows, a way-out piano player who answered "cool" to anything that was said, and a man on sax who really turned me on—Sam "The Man" Taylor. Sam just sat there warming up, looking into his sax, and taking long gulps on a bottle of booze at his side. He didn't even know I was in the room, yet all I could think of was the countless records he had made. Even bad records benefited from Sam's "fender" (rock talk for the orchestral part of the record). He just lent a little something special to that whole studio.

We started with "Hey Red!" in what I perceived as the most anarchic arrangement possible. At "Now!" everyone commenced, but I didn't hear them, and they didn't hear me. Only an engineer with Cool C glasses borrowed from an old Sid Caesar show seemed to know what was happening. I could tell from the takes that no one was impressed. At take eleven Bobby gave an uninspired "That's it. Wrap that one up." I was sure that on that side Presley's preeminence was not likely to be challenged. On the playback, the only redeeming feature was Sam's solo. His playing made me feel like returning to family reunions. With the intro to "Steady" I relaxed a bit more, and the sounds began to come easy. At the last refrain, when the key changed, I really had a chance to wail. I just didn't want the music to end. On the playback even Sam applauded. He walked over and said, "Kid, that song ain't much, but you did all anybody could do with it."

I was in the business. Between classes I read *Variety* and

anticipated my calculatedly cool response to Hollywood overtures. I was also about to be introduced to the harsh realities that separated me, and my generation, from sixties innocence.

Since everything had gone so smoothly, I hadn't, as yet, seen the advantage of recording for a big company; but I was soon to find out the hard way. It's not easy to cut a record, but it's next to impossible for a small company to distribute it and get it aired. Payola in the fifties had one virtue: there was no deception. One gave a disc jockey between $1000 and $1500, depending on his station and reputation. There was no conversing; it was a straight and silent business transaction. I quickly learned how a star was born; mine, unfortunately, was falling from the sky.

I did get a few plays on WLIB, probably because someone was convinced I was local soul material. Several Baltimore and Detroit stations also gave the record a chance, but aside from Columbia basketball pre-game warm-ups and the juke-box in the student lounge, my record made it big only at family gatherings and at a remote girls' camp in New York State. I ended up where I started: the family's entertainer and an aging camp heartthrob.

I did emerge from the experience somewhat wiser, convinced of my singing ability, and infinitely more modest than in my Presley imitation days. I could also relive my experience on every date and could play the role of a rock has-been at nineteen. That role I played beautifully. When I did my fraternity bits, I was introduced as that former rock star who recorded on the Buzz label. At camp "We're Not Going Steady" would be played at every dance and I would make a "guest appearance" amid thunderous applause. Hollywood it wasn't, but I enjoyed the attention, even if it came from a captive audience.

Several years later, as I was standing still on the Long
Island Expressway—which happens to be the normal driving speed—I was listening to a crazy disc jockey who had a
program devoted to records that were "not quite gold."
"Next," he said, "is a cut by a guy who played basketball
and could really wail. Where are you now, Herb London?"
I lowered the windows of my car as quickly as I could and
screamed, "Here!" A guy standing next to me yelled back,
"If your car's overheated, why don't you use the highway
phone?" "No, you've got the wrong idea," I answered. "That
guy on the radio wanted to know where I am. He's playing
my record. Listen, that's me." But the guy turned to his
companion and said, "He's daffed. That's what comes from
driving on this expressway."

At that exact moment my musical fantasies ended. Just as
I was being rediscovered, I was caught in a traffic jam and
dismissed as a quack. My most mellifluous tones were being
drowned out by the roar of overheated motors. I was convinced that the world was unfair. That one airing should not
have made that much difference, but if there was any justice
in the world, that playing should rightfully have occurred
as I casually turned on the radio after a nightcap with a
girlfriend. But to be sitting helplessly in a car beseeching
strangers to listen to the radio was enough to convince me
that when things have a chance to go wrong, they generally
do.

This experience had a tremendous impact on my I.C.
When, by the 1960's, every kid with a guitar and a raspy
voice was thinking of himself as a rock performer, I could
sit back and say, "I remember when." It wasn't really a
sense of superiority; it was just the knowledge that making
it wasn't so easy and that, for those who did make it, the
price of getting there was very high indeed. I.C. types have

few illusions about success. We want it, of course. But we also understand that the road is a difficult one. We reject the soft rhetoric which claims that everyone can be successful, and we are contemptuous of the line that success isn't worth pursuing. To us, Dale Carnegie and Eric Bentley seem hopelessly naive.

What did characterize my very limited career were dreams of grandeur deflated by harsh facts. One sniff of the real world sent me reeling. I wanted what every young man wants: success, fame, wealth—all without much effort. I grew up as "We're Not Going Steady" went steadily into oblivion. My experience had taught me that social mobility was more possible than my father had assumed and less possible than David Cassidy fans believe. But getting there demands persistence. Perhaps that explains why I.C. isn't understood by the social dropout who goes the commune route or the beat poet who ends up in a Warner Brothers stable. It's easy to be a success at seventeen—the tough competition has not yet set in. Once past that age, however, nothing comes cheaply.

I.C. is suspicious of non-zero-sum games. In its cosmology, everyone doesn't win. You may decide to change the rules and give every student an A—a practice that is now gaining currency—but whether one likes it or not, qualitative judgments about ability will be made. Similarly, one may argue against the game of advancement-mobility-success; yet, with or without the players, the game goes on.

I wanted people to know I could sing. I wanted recognition. I also knew that someone with few connections, little money, and less influence had a slim chance of getting a fair shake. But I also recognize that no system is entirely equitable, and, while this one needs a hell of a lot of improving, I'm not yet ready for Molotov cocktails or a bucolic setting in the hinterland. I.C. is not an answer to the achievement blues; it is merely a response to the New Deal generation, which wears security as a badge, and the sixties set, which worships at the shrine of inertia.

CHAPTER 3

What It Meant to Be a Fifties Jock

A STORY CONTINUES to circulate that when I was two months old, my parents could keep me quiet only by putting a ball in my crib. Whether this is true or not I am unable to say, but I did carry a ball wherever I went until I was fifteen. The ball was my security blanket, my source of entertainment, my crystal ball of heroic deeds. I could make that ball curve in any direction or even come back to me if I pressed my knuckles into the soft rubber in the right way. Almost any kid brought up on Brooklyn streets could do the same thing, but he probably didn't share my obsession. I was an artist with a "spaldeen" (the usual pronunciation of the Spaulding ball). I relived the Giant-Dodger 1951 playoff series thousands of times by simply throwing a ball against the wall, except that in *my* third game Bobby Thomson didn't hit *the* home run. I was obviously a diehard Brooklyn Dodger fan. The game I replayed more than any other was the second playoff game of that series, which the Dodgers won at the Polo Grounds by a score of 10–0 with Jackie Robinson hitting two home runs. For me, the playoffs ended right there; everything else that happened was too painful to remember.

When I was old enough to travel alone on the subway, I would go to Ebbetts Field three hours before the game so that I might play stickball with Duke, Gil, or some other Dodger who was on his way to the ballpark. But even if no one was around, I could get hours of pleasure simply by throwing a ball at a box drawn on a schoolyard wall. I would practice my curve, knuckler, change of pace, and "smoke" with the 1949 All-Star teams. And all the while I'd announce the results. To this day I don't know why I had to scream at the top of my lungs: "Up first for the Brooklyn Dodgers is the second baseman Junior Gilliam. . ." The mother of Wally, a friend, was convinced I'd either be a baseball announcer or a fishmonger. Announcements lent my mythical games a certain excitement. Invariably the game was won by my favorite team and special hero in the ninth inning; if dinner wasn't ready, the final result might be delayed for several extra innings.

Even while I watched games on television, I would simulate base hits with the ever-present "spaldeen." I used to pepper the wall adjacent to the television set the way Stan Musial hit rifle shots at the nearby right field fence in Ebbetts Field. When I was involved in organized games, that rubber ball usually served me well. I played punchball with a fury that Vince Lombardi would have envied. There was no sentiment when I played. If you could do the job, I wanted you on my team; if not, my opponents were welcome to have you. When my fifth-grade team lost the championship in the final game, I cried for six hours. Yet I loved competition. I would rise to the occasion in the big game or against the top-ranked opponents. Despite the recent challenge to competitive sports made by Dave Meggysey, Chip Oliver, and George Sauer, I have seen exploits on a playing field that often defied reason. There was undoubtedly a price to be paid for this zealousness: To this day, I am compulsive about success, winning, and rewards. But while I recognize this neurosis, I am convinced that it is not too high a price to pay for the potential benefits. Yet this is merely another critical attitude that sets me apart from the noncompetitive spirit of Woodstock.

When I was twelve, my parents made what was undoubtedly our most significant family move. They decided to leave Brooklyn for Queens. The distance was only a matter of twenty miles, but no move could have been more important. We were leaving a $32-a-month two-room flat for a four and one-half room apartment whose rent was $99 a month. All I kept asking about, at first, was: what is half a room? I never did get a satisfactory answer, but that hardly mattered, especially when I saw my own bedroom for the first time. Then I knew why everyone made a big deal about Moses leading the Jews out of Egypt. The new apartment in Kew Garden Hills really wasn't much—a three-flight walk-up, with bicycles in the front entrance, and ubiquitous flies near the garbage wells in the ground —but for me it was a promised land.

Yet a move of this kind also had its drawbacks. I didn't know anyone; since I never spoke to strangers, I wasn't likely to get to know anyone either. For the first two weeks I just ran to my new school and back home—a distance of about a mile—without so much as staring at a face. When I did begin to communicate it was not with words, but

29

with my "spaldeen." I hit it harder, threw it farther, or pitched it faster than most other boys. That ball was usually my card of introduction to strangers.

My first teacher was a young fellow who had played with the successful City College basketball teams of the late forties and early fifties. We rarely spoke to one another, but he nonetheless gave me many lessons on a basketball court. Basketball was certainly not my first love, but I was clearly suited for it. I was the tallest boy in my class, with colt-like legs which were perfect for running and hands that responded well to quickly thrown balls. Before the year was out basketball had become my favorite sport, and I was uttering sounds that only faintly resembled words.

By the time I graduated from junior high school, I was the second highest scorer in the league and just about tops in every other category for which statistics were kept. I still spoke infrequently, but that hardly made a difference. I was president of my class, considered one of the brightest students in the school and, most important, the only person who obtained every student signature for his graduation yearbook. Yet all I could think of during the graduation ceremony was playing high school basketball. For me that was the big time.

Although I lived on the imaginary boundary separating school districts, I was assigned to Jamaica High School instead of the one in Forest Hills. The decision annoyed my folks but pleased me; my schoolyard experience had convinced me that an integrated high school, which Jamaica was at the time, was more likely to have a good basketball team—nothing could be more important than that. But, as with most sports freaks, my life-style changed with each change in the sports season. With the start of the first football exhibition in August, I got my pigskin out of the closet and started to practice.

That month in 1956 was particularly eventful: I was getting ready to enter high school, while serving as quarterback on a football team in the Pop Warner league. Because my team practiced day and night, I had little time to think about high school or basketball. Since I was convinced of my indestructibility—a condition symptomatic of adolescence—I never wore shoulder pads when I played. I contended that they interfered with my passing accuracy. I soon found out why everyone else wore pads when they played. One week before school was to begin and our first game was to be played, I fractured my left shoulder during football practice. Aside from the pain and the discomfort associated with a cast, I didn't give the matter much thought—until I read about tryouts for the high school junior varsity basketball team. Since Jamaica had no football team, basketball practice started early; so did my depression. I just moped around the school and the house every day. Occasionally I'd take my basketball out of the closet and dribble around the house, to the consternation of my mom and our downstairs neighbors. But that was a poor substitute for getting out on the court.

My spirits perked up somewhat when I learned that only one freshman had made the jay vees, and he didn't even have any prospect of playing. From the very outset, the coach was apparently intent upon introducing humility. His method for doing so was simple: freshmen didn't make the team; sophomores played with the jay vees; and juniors sat and watched seniors play. The strategy usually worked to the disadvantage of extremely talented players, but the coach's teams always won. I've found that most people don't argue with success. I had no way of knowing whether

I could have made that freshman team, but I had several handy rationalizations to mitigate the possibility of failure.

On my way to and from school, I imagined myself on an extended fastbreak. I would feint passersby by pretending to dribble a basketball; at the No Parking sign on the corner I would, to the general delight of the crowd, stuff the ball. I could hear the gymnasium ringing with cheers, but the man-on-the-street was convinced that I needed shock therapy. Mrs. Saks, a neighbor in our building, would ask my mother if I was okay. "He has such funny motions," she would say with her usual discretion.

Just as I had once carried my "spaldeen" with me at all times, I now carried a basketball. I would dribble it through my legs, pass it over my shoulder, watch it spin on one finger, and bounce it off my head and into a hoop. I thought I could simulate any move by the Harlem Globetrotters. By acclamation I was voted all-schoolyard—which merely meant that I was selected first in any choose-up game. I was also growing; at thirteen I was over six feet tall and by fifteen I was six feet four inches. Coaches used to stare at my feet and make strange nodding gestures with their heads. I wore a size fourteen sneaker.

By the time my sophomore year began, I thought I was ready for the junior varsity tryouts. The fact was, other guys were more ready than I was, and less cocky. Everything I did at the tryout was wrong, although I did the wrong things with a flare. The Coach must have been impressed by something I did because I made the team, but I made it by a very slim margin. There was no jubilation over that success; I wanted to play and I knew I'd be relegated to the bench.

For the first few games of the season, I sat and watched.

Then I went home, grunted a lot, and drowned my sorrows in a quart of milk and a whole marble loaf. Finally, as in the Chip Hilton stories I had read repeatedly, I got my chance. We were playing Forest Hills and the gym was packed; for a junior varsity game to attract such a turn-away crowd was certainly unusual. The game was even and relatively uneventful until our center picked up his fourth foul. With five minutes left, I was sent in. I didn't hear any of the instructions the coach gave me. As he swatted me on the butt, I swallowed my gum. For several seconds I just stood there, choking as inconspicuously as I could while the public address system let everyone know the name of the tall kid with the tearful eyes. In the game, though, I played like a giant bird, blocking every shot at the hoop. For basketball aficionados there is no move more exciting than the big "B" (blocked shot); the cheering I heard came from keen basketball observers. We won the game. I earned more playing time, the first page in my scrapbook was filled, and I had been given a nickname—"the Kangaroo."

I could go to the boards; rebounding was my forte. I loved the sound of bodies slamming off my back as opponents vainly tried to get the ball which nestled securely in my right hand. I got a charge out of scoring, but this was nothing compared to the big rebound. Lots of guys could score, but no one could do it without the ball—and I got the ball. Coach (in basketball lingo "Coach" is not preceded by a definite article; it stands alone, like God) recognized my special talent and let me play more often than I had expected during my junior year. That year our team won the city championship, a feat recognized by half the schoolyard population of New York as the zenith in sports achievement.

For two weeks in succession my teammates and I did nothing but eat. Dinners were given by the Chamber of Commerce, an alumni association, various all-star groups, parents, girlfriends, and grandmothers. But the experience that meant the most to me was getting the city championship sweater. It was a white cardigan with a red, white, and blue championship patch on one sleeve and gold stars on the other. In my senior year only two guys had that sweater. It was my calling card at parties, my invitation to join a fraternity, and my magnet for girls. Almost half the five thousand students at Jamaica High School had visions of wearing that sweater. I intended to give each and every one of those girls an opportunity to try it on.

Senior year was more serious than other years. I now had a chance to establish my own basketball credentials and, in so doing, win a college scholarship. I had the grades to enter the City University, which charged no tuition, but I sought something better. College tuition rates, even in the fifties, were high enough for my dad to start campaigning for Queens College as the best choice. "You'll be a big fish in a little pond," he said. "Yeah, sure, Dad, sure," I mumbled. Something more, I felt, was in store for me.

My dad, something of a basketball freak himself, screamed louder than anyone at games and took some of the losses as hard as I did. But my mom never really understood or cared about what was happening. "Why make such a fuss over a beach ball?" she would ask me. The advice was better than I realized at the time. Nevertheless, I finally convinced her to attend the second game of the season against Forest Hills, our arch rival. The stands, as was often the case, were filled to capacity; approximately two thousand people were at that game. And there, prominently placed in the third row, were my parents. I obviously wanted to impress them.

As I have discovered time and again, excessive zeal usually ensures failure. This was just such a case. I was lousy; my shots missed, I was lackadaisical on defense, and the ball always seemed to be bouncing away from me. But the worst was still to come. In the last quarter, with four minutes remaining, someone stuck his finger in my eye. Nothing serious, mind you; it was the kind of injury that warrants one minute's inattention from the coach. As my eyes closed for an instant, I could have sworn that my mom was on the court asking me if I was all right. I knew that it couldn't be true, so I didn't give the matter a second thought. But when I opened my eyes, my worst fears were realized: there she was, attending to my eye in front of two thousand people. All I wanted to do was go home and hide in my room for a year or two. At that moment, I thought of disguises I might wear or exotic places in the South Pacific where I might establish permanent residence.

Though I could not forget that nightmarish incident, the fact that the team won fourteen straight games that season, and thirty-three consecutively over a two-year period, made the experience less painful. We were on our way to the New York City record, with but one major hurdle in our path: De Witt Clinton High School. It had already been intimated that *Sport* magazine would carry a feature on our team if we beat Clinton. I had visions of legions of photographers descending on my home, taking pictures of me with captions such as "Herb relaxing at home," "out on a date," "sitting in his tub." But I had no such luck; we lost to Clinton by three points. I still have the suspicion that most of the guys on our team had *Sport* magazine on their minds more than Clinton basketball players. I know I did.

Despite that loss, we tore through our league and went to Madison Square Garden for the city quarter finals with a nineteen and two record. Playing before sixteen thousand screaming people was enough to have me biting my fingernails down to the cuticle before the game even started. From all the telephone calls my folks made, I was sure that at least a quarter of the crowd was comprised of family and friends. My dad even got the day off to attend the game, an event without precedent in his life. As sports buffs would say, our supporters were not disappointed; we put it all together. We won by twenty-seven points in what was supposed to be a closely contested game. My own statistics were equally impressive: sixteen points and fifteen rebounds in the first half (all the regulars were seated during the second half). Now that we were the Queens champions, all we had to do was defeat Boys' High in order to get to the city finals. Almost everyone who saw us play was convinced that we'd be home free if we could only beat that team.

There was a certain mystique about Boys' High. Allegedly, everyone who made that team could dunk, even the guys under five feet seven. And those over six foot three dunked two balls in rapid succession without touching the ground. Opponents were often intimidated before the game even began. And when the bongos started to play, you knew that the B-O-Y-S cheer would commence amid a reverberating crash of deafening and frightening sounds. That team was so good that the *sixth* man was Lennie Wilkins—the same Wilkins who became All-American at Providence and a perennial All-Pro after 1961.

The day before the game against Boys' High, I sprained my ankle during practice. The swelling was severe enough to completely conceal the ankle bone. Yet when Coach asked about it, I said it was nothing that a hot bath couldn't cure. Unwilling to accept answers he didn't expect, he decided not to press the matter. By the time I limped home, my dad had already made an appointment with the doctor. During the next twenty-four hours that ankle was submerged in a whirlpool for a good three-quarters of the time. I was beginning to feel like Marat, although my objective was obviously more limited than revolution: I simply wanted to be able to play. I would have sold my soul and anything else of value to the devil for one hour without that balloon around my ankle bone. I'm not trying to build myself up as some kind of a martyr; but, after all those games and personal expectations, the thought of sitting on the bench and watching someone play in my place was just too much for my seventeen-year-old emotions to bear.

I did play, although I never matched the level of my previous performance. But Boys' High was also less than I had expected. We were behind by ten at the half, but I now knew that those guys were less than supermen. In the second half we closed the gap quickly. In fact, with two minutes to go, one of our guys was at the foul line with a chance to tie the game. The shot was soft and right on the rim, but for an instant it remained in suspension. Eyeing that ball, I instinctively jumped and slammed it in. Just as I did, the referee blew his whistle: I was apparently guilty of offensive interference. My eagerness not only cost us the point and gave the ball to Boys' High, it probably also cost us the entire game. We lost by one point. In an instant the season was at an end. It was not the kind of ending I had read about in Chip Hilton stories.

No sooner had the season ended than I was besieged with offers of college scholarships. I ate at Mamma Leone's so often that even after I had brushed my teeth five times a day, my breath still smelled of garlic. I spoke to so many businessmen that the two suits in my wardrobe acquired a pungent cigar aroma. Talent scouts appeared from nowhere; my mom found herself preparing snacks for the uninvited guests almost every night. I received assurances from the coach at Toledo University that a chauffeur-driven car would be in front of my house to take me to the campus and drive me back, *with no strings attached.* I really did want to see Toledo, but no one was going to get me to attend that college. Still, the idea of a chauffeur taking me everywhere was enough to swell my head to the size of a watermelon.

Having learned, after years of reading *Sport* magazine articles, that athletes are often exploited, I wanted a college that was interested in more than just my body, although I must admit that I was interested in little more than the college's gymnasium. My choices were finally narrowed down to New York University (it played its home games in Madison Square Garden), Dartmouth (it was recruiting some of the best basketball players in the city), and Columbia (Lou Gehrig went there). I think Columbia became my first choice when the coach, who happened to be Italian, didn't take me to Mamma Leone's for dinner. My dad also had confidence that a Columbia degree was "worth more"—more what he couldn't say—than one from the other contending colleges. When the Columbia coach asked me what I wanted to study, I hesitated before answering pre-med. In fact, I didn't know that Jewish males had an option. Besides, there was nothing in the Columbia curriculum called pre-basketball.

When I arrived at Columbia College, wearing my undersized and ridiculous freshman beanie, I felt as awkward as any high school jock possibly could, but I thought that the transition from high school to college would not be so difficult. My roommate was a long-time friend and a basketball player. I had a lucrative scholarship that immediately set me apart. I still had my white city championship sweater which I always wore when I needed to boost my confidence. Yet that first year turned out to be as bad as I had feared it would, and then some. I realized that I had problems when I saw a mass of little kids (they couldn't have been more than fifteen) from the Bronx High School of Science carrying test tubes at freshmen orientation. It wasn't that I had any particular prejudice against test tubes, Bronx Science, or fifteen-year-olds; I just felt that these guys would soon be looking through the wrong end of a microscope. I also discovered that the job I had secured through the Coach, which I envisioned as a sinecure, turned out to be a back-breaking job serving food in the cafeteria. I had a schedule that would have challenged the energy of an anal compulsive on Benzedrine. I attended classes from nine A.M to twelve; I worked from twelve to three; I had a class from three to four; from four-thirty to seven-thirty I practiced basketball; dinner lasted till eight-thirty; and *then* I started to study. I ran everywhere that year, but I felt as if I were caught on a treadmill.

Just as I would begin to think that I could cope with all my roles, something would inevitably set me back. First, there was an automobile accident, in which I sustained seven stitches and a shaved scalp. Needless to say, the latter was by far the more severe injury. I practiced basketball while wearing a hat, and even wore it in games. Then, as soon as my hair started to grow back, I became aware of the fact that I had no aptitude whatsoever for chemistry. It wasn't the formulas that threw me, it was the lab. I had a phobia about Bunsen burners and test tubes and possessed about as much mechanical aptitude as Mighty Joe Young. I still hold the Columbia record for the largest one-semester payment for broken lab equipment. Rather than go through the ordeal of burned fingers and mini-explosions, I would break a key piece of equipment. In my year of chemistry I never once had a fellow student work next to me. I was the scourge of the lab. Even when I did complete an experiment, which was rare, the results would defy the lab assistants. They would look at me and say, "London, you didn't clean your test tubes thoroughly." The next week, to avoid ignominy, I would break my test tubes. I received an F for my lab performance, B+ for my classwork and a C for the course. It wasn't the kind of experience that inspired self-confidence.

Initially, my basketball performance was about the only thing that kept me going. But that didn't last long. The freshman coach expected me to be a combination of instant All-American and the Second Coming; but since I only made the All-Queens schoolboy team, I didn't pose an immediate threat to Oscar Robertson's college records. Yet the disparity between his expectations and my ability was enough to bring a scowl to his face at the mere mention of my name. Although I started the first three games, by the third one I wasn't getting much more playing time than the opening tip-off. When I spoke to Coach, he said, "I've got to see more hustle from you in practice." Since we were having an intra-squad scrimmage that day, I went all out.

At the half I had twenty-seven points; in the third quarter, while trying to impress Coach with some fancy-dan dribbling, I was blind-sided by a teammate attempting to steal the ball from me. There was no question about it, my collarbone was broken: I could see the bone.

The collarbone was quickly set and I was fitted into a halter to permit the break to heal. I was beginning to think that somewhere someone was sticking pins into a doll named Herb London. But I was determined to see things through, even if it meant being a permanent Medicare case at seventeen. So, five days after the collarbone was set, I was back serving hash at the cafeteria. Since I rarely spoke, my supervisor didn't even know that I had been injured. I don't think I would have wanted it any other way.

Three months later the halter was removed. I immediately started to take shots in the gym. Although I still had three months of convalescence remaining, the moment Coach asked me when I could resume playing, I replied: "Tomorrow." So, after the trainer had shaved my trunk from neck to waist and applied enough Johnson and Johnson tape to raise the company's stock dividends, I was back on the court. I looked like something out of a Rube Goldberg nightmare. My left arm was useless, I could bend at the waist only at great risk to my lungs, and I ran as if I were the headless horseman. But I was playing—and that was the first upbeat thing that had happened in months. That feeling lasted exactly three days; at a game that weekend I broke the insufficiently healed collarbone.

Before going to bed each night I reread the tale of Job. There had to be a divine will behind my plight. I began to anticipate the evil that would befall me each day. During

41

my frequent visits to the hospital, I experienced a continual phobia about chemistry lab, an advanced state of self-imposed loneliness, a developing state of paranoia, and real doubts about my adequacy. My mental health was not so different from my physical well-being (the term should read "poor-being"). Although everyone had told me that college would be a learning experience, I never expected an all-expenses-paid tour through purgatory.

Although I never could embrace the power of positive thinking with any degree of enthusiasm, I did decide that some positive changes in my life were needed. Of course, that astute observation was no better than telling Rip Van Winkle he could have used an alarm clock. I faced up to my laboratory woes by switching my major to history; I also vowed not to engage in a historical examination of the Bunsen burner. I decided that my alleged lack of aggressiveness on the basketball court could be remedied by means of a rigorous weight lifting program. And I was sure that my spirits could be lifted if I only had some romance. The results of my efforts were quite remarkable. History put basketball in its proper perspective and, for the first time, made it seem relatively insignificant. Weight lifting gave me a sense of self-awareness and humility. Romance made me less humble and destroyed my perspective on everything.

When the next basketball season began, I vowed to be philosophical about my fate. I was assured of making the varsity, but since the coaching staff relied equally on rumor and performance to determine who played, I knew I would be at a disadvantage. The rap against me was that I was sometimes lackadaisical and injury-prone. On the basis of what had happened the previous year, the claims were at least partially true. Yet my career had, until that year, moved in just the opposite direction. That fact apparently meant little or nothing to those who asked, "What have you done lately?" It was equally apparent that most basketball coaches were not history majors.

In the very first scrimmage of the year, I scored seventeen points and grabbed twenty-three rebounds. Coach, who was as generous with compliments as Scrooge, casually suggested, at the next practice, that I keep it up. Presumably, the comment was designed as a confidence builder, but it didn't have that effect on me. No matter how well I played in practice, I couldn't overcome my earlier fears. Like many guys who sit on the bench, I thought I deserved to be playing. Although I did get to start a few games, and performed creditably in several, I was usually yanked as soon as I made one mistake. I began to play with a "one mistake" obsession. Since one bad pass, missed shot, or violation would have meant my departure from the game, I avoided the ball like the plague. As a result, my playing conformed to what I felt was a false image of myself. I played as if I lacked confidence, and, for the first time, I *did* lack a sense of confidence.

Despite everything, I won a letter that year; this, in turn, entitled me to a varsity blazer. Yet even that honor didn't have the same impact on me as the city championship sweater. I visited several interesting places, took my first airplane trip, and watched Coach break folding chairs from Detroit to Cambridge. This last comment undoubtedly needs some explanation. Since the team often lost— a very new experience for me—and since Coach was incapable either of generating a winning attitude or of giving an emotional Knute Rockne half-time speech, he would do his famous destruction-of-a-folding-chair routine during a harangue about our poor defense. It did have

43

something of an emotional flourish to it. The effect was sometimes inspirational; it must have been, for it remains one of the few things about that season I'll never be able to forget.

To my surprise, Coach took himself and his folding-chair routine to New York University the following year. I must confess that I wasn't sorry to see him go. My next coach was six feet eight inches of Caspar Milquetoast. He often described the malted milks his mother prepared for him before he went to bed. He wrote incredible love stories that were published in *Playboy* magazine, and he had his androgynous girl friend keep statistics at our games. His breath was so bad that everyone on the team cupped a hand over his face at team meetings. He even had us practice our formation for the pre-game rendition of "The Star Spangled Banner." During a time-out at one game he got so carried away that he couldn't even recall our names or the team against which we were playing. In so many ways he reminded me of an elongated Captain Queeg rolling basketballs in his hands. Nonetheless, he kept an open mind about who should be playing. From my point of view this one positive trait cancelled out all his other eccentricities.

During the next two basketball seasons, I started every game but the first two. I had moments of embarrassment (missing three uncontested layups in a Dartmouth game) and moments of glory (hitting all my shots against Army and eight consecutive foul shots to defeat Yale). Our team was not what you would call outstanding, but we were in almost every game. In a very short time the rap against me was turned around. Instead of a shirker, I came to be regarded as a supreme hustler. Rudy LaRusso, later of N.B.A. fame, once said I was the toughest defensive center he had to face. And Leroy Ellis, first connected with St. Johns and later a member of the Los Angeles Lakers, once threatened to kick me in the balls if I didn't stop hustling. Actually, I wasn't playing differently; I just had the feeling that I wouldn't be taken out of the game if I made a mistake. It was an important lesson for me. Success, I'm convinced, is mainly a function of confidence, and confidence comes from knowing someone will stay with you even if you make a mistake.

For me, sports represent a classic metaphor of American life. But they are more than that; they represent the essential building block of I.C. At a time when shirkers are often admired and success is considered a dubious distinction, I find myself quite out of place. My athletic experience taught me a very important lesson: to "win," you have to play "the game." My obsession with sports was very much a process of imbibing social rules. Playing the game meant working hard, overcoming obstacles, building up confidence in oneself. There are undoubtedly emotional trials and tense moments in sports, but these are the very challenges that help a man (or woman) find out what he (or she) can do. To dismiss them as too rigorous is to ignore one's own potential. During one of my frequent weight lifting sessions I discovered a curious way of testing one's mettle. There were others who could flamboyantly lift two hundred and fifty or even three hundred pounds, a feat I at first thought was amazing. But the people I truly came to admire were those who, though thoroughly exhausted, still managed to execute one more press with a one hundred or a fifty pound weight, the ones who could push themselves to the limits of their endurance. Such athletes came in all sizes; in fact, physical appearance was an inaccurate way of judging them.

I have no way of knowing, but I suspect that these are the people who get the most out of what they do. To the children of affluence, "the plugger" seems an anachronism, a rate-buster of the uptight fifties. Conversely, the plugger views the seventies as a decade of voracious appetites, a time when the feasting is easy. In fact, while the Woodstock Nation opts out of the "rat race," the plugger is busy building mouse traps. Oscar Handlin once said, "The toughness of the times is the flabby alibi for the under-achiever." Handlin has perfectly captured the spirit that sports provoked in me.

Today, college basketball games attract a handful of students, even if the teams are first-rate. I've been told sports are "hokey," that it's really much better to turn on. Obviously, the young are being socialized differently, and that explains why I don't relate to their culture. It should also be obvious that my parents' generation, which was socialized during the Depression, is equally peculiar to me. Sports meant taking calculated risks; it often meant doing the unexpected. Tom Rath was too damned predictable; from my rather narrow perspective, he was a product of an overwrought concern for security. Like almost all my previous experiences, I perceive my athletic activity as having been instrumental in molding my I.C. attitude. Had I attended college at an earlier point in my life, I undoubtedly would have rejected sports as a diversion intended only for spoiled rich kids. And had I been of college age in the sixties, I probably would have repressed my athletic inclinations for fear of being labeled a "jock" (read: mindless athletic freak).

My socialization through sports turned out to be more important than the events themselves. Anything could happen in a game; the element of chance often altered the plans of even the most well-prepared athlete. In retrospect, the anticipation, the learned behavior, and the dedication to the event seemed to be what really mattered most. Practice was not a meaningless ritual; it was *the* lesson of sports. Joe Namath may call practice bullshit, but that explains why he is Joe Namath and not Whizzer White.

Even today, when I pick up a newspaper, I read the sports pages first. The best way I can explain this choice is to quote a statement by Earl Warren, the former Chief Justice, who said, "I like to read about man's accomplishments before I get to his failures." But I'm still obsessive, as are most I.C. products. I can always identify as a confrere the person who memorizes, for no apparent reason, the batting averages of the top twenty hitters in either baseball league or the number of rebounds Wilt Chamberlain averaged per game last year. I still get a charge when I meet someone who saw me play basketball in high school or college. And I share, along with other I.C. products, a strangely ecstatic feeling when I hold a ball in my hands. Stranger yet, I watch football and basketball games on television even when they are uninteresting. For me, those games, even the boring ones, capture a spirit of pure competition that neither my parents nor my children can understand. In my moments of pure fantasy, I am once again playing college basketball—yes, with all its pain—except that the perspective is a bit clearer in the replay. With what I now know, it wouldn't make that much difference if, in my daydreams, I was relegated to the bench. For I finally understand that my generational view was based on a convention of athletic challenge that went beyond the individual encounter. I didn't know it then—I couldn't; it was pre-I.C.

CHAPTER 4
The End of Idealism

TEACHING WAS MY ATTEMPT at digging political trenches for my personal war against the insensitive and the unfeeling. I was going to make this a better world—almost any cliché of the sixties can be substituted—by reaching those who were supposed to be directing the future of our nation. I was armed for the task with little more than my idealism and several clichés preempted from one of the early books on radical school reform. Still, I believed I could reach kids, particularly poor black kids. To champion the cause of kids was not a sign of sufficient liberalism; you had to be for poor black kids. Teaching was also a battleground where I could find out more about myself. It was a test of mettle in the same way—or so I thought —as joining the International Brigade had been a personal test of courage for an earlier generation. But it wasn't only idealism that sent me into the schools—I didn't know what else to do with myself. The romantic battle analogy was a most appropriate rationalization; at twenty-one, although I had sufficient idealism, I had no career aspirations whatsoever.

When I told a so-called college advisor that I had no interest in medicine, my declared major, yet didn't know what else to do, he suggested that I take something called the Kuder Preference Test. So I diligently arranged for this test of my presumptive interests. Several hours later I discovered that I'd prefer to be a circus performer as opposed to a forest ranger. I also received other enlightening bits of information, such as my preference for indoor versus outdoor occupations. When I asked for an interpretation of these results, a vocational counselor sputtered and said, "You prefer to work with people rather than things." Whereupon I asked who worked with things. I was subsequently sent on my way as an ungrateful student. It was the kind of response I came to expect from advisors and counselors.

When I really thought about it—which wasn't too often —I realized that summer camp was usually a delightful interlude in an otherwise hectic year. It was a time to bronze my skin, be irresponsible, keep a casual vigil vis-à-vis spoiled fifteen-year-olds, and engage in a seemingly unending series of athletic events. I was also not so naive as to believe that I could do this all year long, much less past my twenty-first birthday. I had been to enough camps to know that there are few things quite so pathetic as an aging camp counselor. However, the job that seemed most closely related to this camp life was teaching. Besides, since I had no discernible aptitude (aside from an alleged preference for working with people), I was, from my own observation, an eminently desirable teaching candidate.

After graduating from college I enrolled in an M.A.

program, sponsored by the Board of Education, which granted college graduates lacking education credits permission to teach in the city schools. As one of those teachers, I soon realized that my "opportunity" meant combat duty on St. Nicholas Avenue. I also came to realize that, radical school reformers to the contrary, the rationale behind the need for education courses can probably be justified. I had a textbook knowledge of the history that I was trying to teach, but I related "the facts" with as much flair as a census officer reading the *Statistical Abstract*. After spending two days in an all-girls junior high school, I was sure that the kids would have me impaled on the schoolyard flagpole within two weeks. These girls were more than hardened, they were sadistic. From the moment each class began until the final bell, these kids used every conceivable mental torture in their considerable repertoire to break my will. Since I was still an idealist, I maintained that their previous social conditioning would not inhibit my creativity. I would make them learn—and like it, too.

My first ploy was a simple Pavlovian experiment. Having learned that these kids loved pickles—I had almost broken my back by stepping on a discarded pickle in my classroom—I bought thirty-five pickles and proceeded to distribute them to those who performed well. This worked beautifully for the first five minutes, or until the pickles were devoured, but after that the girls clamored for more rewards. I always wondered what Pavlov did with his dogs when he ran out of food.

Next, I thought I could generate some interest if I related rock music to history. Through a hand vote—the handmaiden of democracy—I determined the most popular rock tune in the class: a song called "Step by Step."

Then I proceeded to enlist the class's support in writing new lyrics to the tune which related to the subject I had been teaching. In two sessions "Step by Step" was trans-formed to read:

> Step by step Hitler fell in love with you
> and step by step he engulfed you, too.
> First step, he called it lebensraum.
> Second step was taking town after town.
> Third step, he invaded the Rhine.
> Fourth step, the allies bided their time.
> Fifth step, Chamberlain met him in Munich.
> Sixth step, Sudetenland was broken like a stick.
> Seventh step, he said he had his fill.
> Eighth step, his troops cracked the Polish will.
> Step by step these events began the war.
> And step by step as we gave, Hitler wanted more.

You would have to know the melody to appreciate this obviously simplistic lesson. Yet it worked. To my delight the kids came to school humming this song each day. Finally, a mid-year exam was given. Since I could contribute one question to the test, I naturally asked what events preceded the beginning of World War II. When my students saw this question, they were so thrilled they could barely stop singing. In fact, that is precisely what they did—sing. They insisted on singing their answers. Since the proctor was not accustomed to a singing mid-year exam, my students were dismissed, the class failed the exam, and I was reprimanded for using an inappropriate teaching method.

Undaunted, I came up with another technique for generating interest. I recalled a biological principle—"ontogeny recapitulates phylogeny"—that I thought had some application in my classroom, even if the idea had already been discarded by biologists. If the development of an

51

individual is related to the history of the species, I reasoned, then history and the social sciences can be taught through the experiences of students. The theory was unimpeachable. Years later I even discovered that this is the ostensible feature of the "inductive approach" to teaching. But I wasn't employing pretentious ideas because educators had discovered them. I simply wanted to get my students involved. So I began each lesson by asking them to tell me about their experiences. Invariably their responses dealt with sex; it was the one common concern in the class. My students really were thrilled to learn about the promiscuity of Catherine the Great. But that's all they wanted to talk about. We spent weeks discussing the sexual prowess of Napoleon, Mussolini, Harding, and, of course, Henry VIII. I could only wonder where this was all leading. Of course, it is natural for adolescents to be interested in sex, but these kids had a special reason for their preoccupation. During the half-year I taught in the school, half the thirteen-year-olds in my eighth-grade class became pregnant. That, by the way, may also have been an explanation for their love of pickles.

I spent every free moment I had doing research on the sexual habits of famous historical figures. I certainly learned some things that could have improved Woody Allen's film version of *Everything You Always Wanted to Know About Sex* . . . and so did my students. But when my colleagues inquired about the enthusiasm of my classes, the answer they received was "sex." Since I wasn't supposed to be teaching Health Education, the answer seemed rather strange to the other teachers. In no time at all I was characterized as a pervert in every conversation in the teachers' section of the cafeteria. From pickles to rock and sex, my ideas either failed dismally in the classroom or violated well-established standards of teaching propriety. I wasn't going to leave teaching, not yet anyway, but I was confident that either teaching standards were going to have to be revised or I was going to have to revise *my* teaching standards. The latter seemed a more reasonable alternative.

Since I had had a teaching experience, albeit a truncated one, in an all-girls school, it only seemed reasonable that I should now teach in an all-boys school. It wasn't that I had any particular concern for balancing my experience; I wanted to find out if young male students liked pickles as much as their female counterparts. So each morning I traveled to the farthest reaches of the Bronx to get to De Witt Clinton High School. The journey was a test of my commitment to teaching; on rainy winter mornings there was no doubt in my mind that I was more committed to a warm bed than to any youngster, even the one-in-a-million who was eager to learn.

My job at Clinton was not at all like my earlier experience. Discipline was still something of a problem, but the principal would stand behind your decision to punish a disruptive student. Colleagues would often talk about you in the teachers' cafeteria, but there were some truly extraordinary teachers in the school. Getting students involved led me to try some very unorthodox approaches, e.g., wearing a raccoon coat and a skimmer when I taught about the twenties, but the reactions were generally muted and, as a consequence, my actions were less controversial. The factor that made my six-month employment memorable was another teacher. He was one of the crassest, sloppiest, most insulting and brilliant people one is likely to meet in a public school system. He was also one of the most effective teachers.

Jerry violated every prescription in the Board of Education guidelines. He intimidated students, lectured to them, forced them to work above their level, and wore an outfit that could only have been purchased at a Bowery sale. Kids loved him. They raced to his classes only to hear him bellow, "Refugees from humanity, today I will try to bring you *up to* the Neanderthal stage of your development." When someone gave him a wrong answer, he screamed, "Every time you open your mouth you subtract from the sum total of human knowledge." Yet despite the insults (or perhaps because of them), these kids, none of whom had expectations of going to college, were reading primary documents that are ordinarily assigned to freshman history students at Harvard. For me, this man was something of a paragon. Every once in a while I unconsciously employ one of his insults to disarm a student, but as soon as I do, a deep, uncontrollable laughter begins.

By the end of my interim appointment I had decided that another change of scenery would be welcome. I had no gypsy blood that I knew of; I simply couldn't face the subway rides every morning. I also had what at the time seemed like a golden opportunity—a chance to teach bright high school kids history through the Great Books series. Yet this experience, though it started out as a quite promising prospect, turned out to be my undoing. After two years, not only was I soured on public schools, but I was secure in the knowledge that teaching in secondary schools was not an occupation for which I was at all suited.

This brief history of opportunity and decline started out auspiciously enough when I entered a high school on the North Shore of Long Island—only to be informed that it was the wrong school. As the events suggest, I would have been better off if I had stayed put. When I finally did find the school that had hired me, I learned that my program included three honors classes and two "track three" classes. (Track three, for the uninitiated, are classes for dull students or for those who are so disruptive as to appear dull.) I thought I was hired to introduce a special course offering for gifted students, but no one, I later learned, teaches the gifted exclusively. Such classes are usually a reward for years of valiant service.

On my very first day in one of my track three classes, I was introduced to "Sage." Sage was anything but sage. His beard was as thick as mine; he always wore a black leather jacket, under which he sported a T-shirt with the sleeves cut off. When, on rare occasions, he *did* take his jacket off, he would just flex his well-developed biceps to give adoring girls a reason to whisper, "Ooh, Sage!" Sage was seventeen and in the tenth grade. He made it that far only because he had promised "to beat the shit out of anyone who failed him." Obviously, on several occasions he had to keep his promise. Sage did no work at school. Yet, despite the fact that he was old enough to leave, he remained; as he put it, "Where would the gang be without me?" As soon as I entered the classroom I was regarded as a threat to Sage's dominance. My size, age, and alleged authority instantly made me a suitable target. I did not have to wait long for the challenge.

"Please be seated," I said in a manner that was firm but not unreasonably harsh. It had taken years to cultivate the right tone for those three words. Everyone responded as I expected he would—a few groans and then the shuffle to his seat—everyone, that is, but Sage. He stood defiantly in the middle of the room and, like a character out of *The Amboy Dukes*, screamed "Fuck you, teach! I ain't

movin', and you and ten like you can't make me." Denying
an urge to punch this punk in the mouth, I replied, "What
will it take to get you to move?" It was an inane rejoinder,
and it gave Sage the upper hand. "If you beat me in an
arm wrestle, I won't mess around." I wanted to refuse;
yet there was so much screaming, and I had handled the
situation so awkwardly, I didn't know what else to do.
Sage was undeniably strong; he also had twenty-five kids
giving him support. For the first ten seconds I was sure it
would be a standoff—which would have been a symbolic
loss for me. But, like John Garfield in one of his vintage
films, I summoned strength I didn't even know I had; I also
cheated by supporting myself with the left hand supposedly concealed behind my back. Sage's hand went down,
and my spirits went up. I felt, for an instant anyway,
that maybe good guys can win occasionally. For perhaps
five seconds I kept Sage's hand pinned to the desk, just to
let him know that I had passed his test; from now on he
had better pass mine.

Word of this so-called feat spread so quickly that, two
periods later, kids were passing my room saying, "That's
the cat who did it." It was certainly a curious development. I had wanted to teach about the Greeks, but I ended
up performing in my own olympics. I also found that
track three classes were more enjoyable than I had expected. Since these kids had no college aspirations, we
chatted about everything. In fact, to this day I can't describe the curriculum of that course. They weren't trying to
justify their mental abilities, as were their gifted counterparts; they had been led to believe—and in some cases
deservedly so—that their mental capacities were limited.
By the end of that year, I was reasonably satisfied with my
position, relatively popular with the students, and some-

what satisfied with the innovations I had introduced. I had, moreover, been given an enthusiastic endorsement by the administration. And I had discovered a member of the teaching staff who was a Long Island version of Portnoy's Monkey, an attractive colleague who could attend to my physical needs. In short, the school presented a comfortable situation in every respect; it was one of the few jobs that I looked forward to retaining for a while.

As I was sitting at my desk during the second year, dreaming lascivious thoughts about one of my students, an anonymous messenger left a note near my arm and departed. No introduction preceded this curious scene, just a note marked "Confidential." It read:

Dear Herb,
We would like to chat with you about your teaching and reading assignments. Please attend the next Board meeting.
Sincerely,
The Superintendent of Schools

I had never met the superintendent; aside from some rumors about his association with well-known local females, he was a complete enigma to me. I thought it surprising that the Board of Education was interested in my teaching, but I truly felt that some of my approaches to teaching deserved commendation. Still, I feared that the Board would not provide a proper setting for the exposure of my ideas. In any case, the matter was academic. Since the meeting was scheduled for the Passover holiday, I did not attend. My refusal was based on the Board's insensitivity rather than my religious observance. However, when I read a transcribed version of the Board "hearing" in a local newspaper, I couldn't believe that the references applied to me. The story read like something out of Arthur Miller's *The Crucible*. For someone who had

57

viewed the Army-McCarthy hearings at an impressionable
age, all I could see before me was an accusatory finger
and a heavily bearded face with bushy eyebrows. The
charges against me were emblazoned on the front page,
next to my picture: 1) Introducing sexually perverse
material, 2) Disregarding various religious views, and
3) Indoctrinating Communist ideology. I concluded that
I had better attend the next Board meeting.

The meeting seemed as anachronistic as hula hoops at
an East Side party. Nonetheless, I found myself face-to-
face with an accuser who had mastered every one of Joseph
McCarthy's techniques. For the Board's information and
mine, Mr. O'Flaherty repeated his charges. "Mr. London
has assigned to his class Sigmund Freud's *The Interpretation of Dreams*, Voltaire's *Candide*, and *The Basic Works
of Communism*. I consider the first sexually perverse, the
second anti-Christian, and the third an insult to American
traditions. Why, just let me read to you from this work."
Mr. O'Flaherty fumbled through several pages and then
began reading from Lenin's "On Revolution." I sat
patiently, but I knew that five minutes of this fiasco was as
much as I could endure. Then O'Flaherty did it. After
stumbling through the most boring passage of an uneven
piece, he cried, "And not only does he assign this trash to
young, impressionable minds, but he does not even attend
the hearing designed to examine the facts. If this isn't a
sign of his guilt, I don't know what is." With that statement, the street fighter in me emerged. To the dismay of
both myself and the superintendent, who had been as sup-
portive as a wet sponge, I screamed:

You narrow-minded schmuck. Sure, I assigned Lenin, Edmund
Burke, D. H. Lawrence, John Stuart Mill, and Djilas. If you would
get your head out of your ass, you would see that I'm less of a

threat to your kid than a *New York Times* editorial or the Declaration of Independence. In fact, if this group of so-called educators can dignify your stupid charges by letting them get into the hands of the local paper and by holding this kind of hearing, this is obviously not a place deserving of some of the modest teaching skill I have demonstrated.

I then left the room, striding off like Emile Zola. In the next hour I hired a lawyer to bring a suit against the local paper, submitted my resignation, and bought an airplane ticket to Europe.

Yet my impulsive actions left me with many doubts. While I felt no obligation to the Board, I did have a well-developed sense of concern for my students. Leaving them before the semester ended did indeed seem an unconscionable act. I also learned from Mr. O'Flaherty's son, who happened to be my poorest student, that his father was often erratic. In the week prior to the alleged hearing, O'Flaherty senior had shaved his son's head, necessitating ten stitches, because junior had let his hair grow below his earlobe. Moreover, while the actions of the Board were inexcusable, and those of the superintendent cowardly, both were under tremendous community pressure from a small but vocal flag-waving, right-wing group that saw the John Birch Society as the last protector of American values. It was rather interesting that O'Flaherty junior, who claimed responsibility for my hearing, initiated it, he later confessed, because the alternative reading to *Candide* (which is on the *Index*) was *Crime and Punishment*, "a book that is two hundred pages longer than the original assignment and a *penalty* for being Catholic."

Since I am now even more moderate (or conservative) than I was then, the incident appears even more ludicrous in retrospect. I could have been charged with indiscreet behavior toward several female students—a charge that would have applied to half the male teaching staff. Or I could have been a target for my sloppy use of language and the curses that slipped out at unguarded moments. Still worse, my informal attire and my disinclination to eat with fellow teachers made me appear bizarre in their eyes. But on these matters, for which I admit guilt, I was not charged.

Despite the anguish, several psychic rewards emerged as a result of the incident. The local newspaper, which was about as responsible as *The National Enquirer*, printed an apology. It appeared on the last page, hidden under an advertisement for suppositories, but, nevertheless, there it was. I'm sure it was a difficult admission to make, but an apology was certainly better than paying off even a portion of my million-dollar lawsuit. My students—who probably enjoyed my classes even more than I thought, and who were inclined to demonstrate in favor of everything from civil rights to the proposed law against the vivisection of dogs—conducted a week-long demonstration in front of the school, accompanied by their parents. I was overjoyed that they considered my fate to be of at least equal importance to the rights of stray dogs. But more important than anything else was my martyrdom. Admittedly, I was a *cause celèbre* for only about two weeks, until the first spring prom, but, within that short time, my conception of myself had altered. I was, or so I thought, the defender of principle fighting against the Philistines. It was a very satisfying position to be in.

About a month after the incident occurred I was on my way to Europe. The flight gave me an opportunity to consider teaching as a career, and to indulge my post-adolescent fantasies about the more cultivated world of Europeans. By the time my plane had landed in London, I had made a firm pledge not to return to public school teaching. For me, the age of idealism terminated at twenty-four. It wasn't just the Long Island neanderthals—they can be found almost anywhere—or the trials with disruptive students; it was the feeling of helplessness that came from trying to do my best, only to find that nothing had changed. Schools are, in my opinion, grossly overrated. Those students likely to succeed in life will do so despite the schools and, in most cases, failure in life cannot be attributed to insufficient school funds or teachers who presumably don't relate. When the public schools were deployed as socializing agents, their function was well understood; indeed, the national values they encouraged were well understood. But the present ferment in national values has obscured the purpose of education. I liked working with adolescents, though certainly not with *all* of them. But there should come a time when teachers aren't didactic, when they aren't just a source of answers to queries about the capital of Uruguay or the best position for sex. That time had come.

Teaching did allow me to clarify the confusion existing in my mind. My I.C. generation of dramatic bus rides and Kennedy clan antics had been overstimulated by the rush of events. The reality of teaching was a chilling yet sobering experience. One fact came home to me: there were no slogans that could solve social woes, even if the words did make one feel better. These were kids, real kids, and some who appeared unreal, each with his own peculiar unreachable past. The fact is, these kids, despite the most turgid claims of educators, could not be reached. Teaching was my confessional, my chance to engage the times. I did so and came out of the experience a better person, I think, although the institutions within which I worked remained unaffected by my efforts. I thought I was trying to save a generation of kids from an insensitive bureaucracy, but, in truth, I was actually trying to work out a personal belief midway between dogma and doubt.

Teaching confirmed I.C. It was an experience that left me with many questions and few answers. All my liberal shibboleths seemed so empty. More money, I had argued, but for what? For better techniques, I had insisted; but who knew what that meant? "Parental participation," the chant of committed radical teachers, became a device for reinstituting every regressive method I thought had been discarded along with Normal Schools. My idealistic fervor was sapped. To hear it all again, a scant ten years later, makes me smile. Wasn't anything learned? Or are I.C. types secretly hoping that youthful idealists will teach in the ghetto schools (for more than a year)? Teaching did bring me to the barricades, both literally and figuratively. At the time, I knew precisely why I was there; the answers seemed so clear. Now, however, the experience exists in my mind only as a fading memory of curious statements, well-meant deeds, and considerable confusion. I dug my trenches, all right, but I certainly did not win any wars; and I positively did not make this a better world. My experience may have made me somewhat wiser, though even that is debatable. It did make me somewhat more realistic. And it reinforced an already developed craving for pickles.

CHAPTER 5

Looking at America from the Other Side of the Globe

As A GRADUATE STUDENT my goal was clear: Do all that was necessary to achieve control over my own time; in other words, work toward a Ph.D. and make my own schedule. Of course, my conception of what one could do with a Ph.D. was drastically revised once I had attained that goal. Nonetheless, I pursued my personal goal for free time with something of a monomaniacal verve and completed the degree in three years. I next wanted to see if this award meant anything more than the teaching certificate that gave me the license to be abused by incorrigible teen-agers. Having based my doctoral research upon a nineteenth-century movement for restrictive immigration in this country, I wanted to find out if there were contemporary illustrations of this restriction elsewhere in the world and, if so, how these states defended their policy against growing international resentment. In effect, I wanted to do a comparative analysis of immigration policies that would enable me to test hypotheses I had explored in one culture and, at the same time, give me an excuse for going abroad, a kind of reward for a year of tedious doctoral research. So, with my recently obtained degree in hand, I applied for a Fulbright grant to Australia to examine "White Australian Policy." It was the first test of the degree's utility, and it passed with flying colors. In August of 1966 I left for the land Down Under.

If there is one country on the globe that bears comparison with the United States, it is Australia. While other nations decry American values and policies, Australians unashamedly embrace them. When I asked an average Australian what he expected from life, he didn't hesitate for a reply: "V.B., tele, and footy." (That's Australian slang or "strine" for Victorian Bitter beer, television, and Australian rules football.) Australians value their comfort and their relatively tranquil life-style. They can be insufferably complacent and charmingly innocent. Despite the radical views of college-age youth, who are amenable to the idealism of the left and are sometimes vigorously anti-American, or those views held by the older patricians, who are self-consciously British and characterize Americans as parvenus, the population is overwhelmingly pro-American. They devour *Playboy*, which, as a result of its alleged lewdness, couldn't be imported until 1970; are avid admirers of American movies; attempt to simulate American eating styles, particularly the hamburger stand (there is no comparison, by the way); can identify with American sports figures; and are as interested in rock music as the average teen-ager from Detroit. Australia was obviously the ideal place for me to evaluate the meaning of American values, to the extent they are discernible there, and, at the same time, evaluate the recent American political and social experience. Australia was an echo that made sounds clearer.

Lest my comments give you the impression that Australia is a mirror image of America, let me note that the Australian people are extraordinarily proud of their nation, much less critical of themselves than are Americans, far more provincial than Yanks, and still have a faith in the working man that has, in recent years, been dissipated here by feather bedding, cynicism about upward mobility, and lassitude encouraged by affluence. In short, Australia is to some extent as idiosyncratic as one could expect. From a parochial American viewpoint, however, one which sees things exclusively in an American context, there are curious parallels to the Midwest of the late forties or early fifties: a period in which fundamentalism still thrived, nationalism prevailed, and a belief in hard work was retained.

I landed in Sydney thoroughly exhausted by the long transoceanic flight but exhilarated by the thought of being so far away from home. My legs were begging for a bed, but my mind wanted to absorb the city as quickly as possible, and my mind won out. I was staying overnight in an area called Kings Cross, which is a cross between the East Village and West Forty-Second Street. It had theaters, dance halls, sailors, fountains, head shops, prostitutes, filth, charm, and overpriced hamburgers. In short, it is ideal for those who do not sleep at night. There is a feeling of bohemian tradition in Kings Cross, somewhat like Soho or Greenwich Village. While the rest of the city is unexceptionable in its respectability, Kings Cross is carefree and even dangerous. The area is also contiguous to Sydney Harbor. When I opened the blinds in the very early morning, I thought someone had pasted a picture postcard scene over my window. The harbor setting was simply glorious: ferries scooting about, the harbor bridge standing like a fortress, the palisades, the blue water, and an incredibly clear sky. Americans often use San Francisco Bay as a standard for urban loveliness, but it doesn't compare with Sydney Harbor. Sydney has a beauty that makes visitors want to return to it again and again. I was certainly no exception. On any free weekend during my stay I could be found strolling on the beach at Bondi or Manley, or sitting on a bluff overlooking the harbor.

Early the next morning I took off for Canberra, the seat of government and location of the national university, my actual destination. From some very hasty examinations of atlases it was clear to me that Australia's capital city was approximately equidistant from Melbourne and Sydney, the major population centers; it was also the only major city not located on the coast. But when the plane landed just past a pasture, I knew I was in the heart of bush country. I had been in remote regions before, but landing in this region of vistas, parched soil, and eucalyptus trees was still a strange sensation to a Brooklyn boy raised on cement. It was clear that Canberra was an architect's dream, a city erected out of empty space surrounded by mountains. It was a place struggling to be born, with magnificent views from every hill and a character as antiseptic as most modern urban architecture.

After a rather tedious orientation session at the university, I was introduced to my advisor. He was a tall man who looked like Walter Pidgeon and talked like Terry Thomas. He radiated all the warmth of Count Dracula. Despite their bravado, Australians are generally uncomfortable in groups outside of a pub. For almost two weeks I went to my assigned office without talking to anyone.

Even during tea breaks (at 10:30 A.M. and 3:30 P.M.) I sipped my tea in complete isolation. Apparently, no one thought it the least bit odd that the newest member of the politics department sat alone. This condition remained unaltered for almost a month. It also prevailed in the rather stodgy place where I resided, a dormitory normally reserved for visiting dignitaries. It had common tables, but I never had any difficulty in eating my meals in utter silence. In fact, the only words I ever spoke were at one of my infrequent invitations to "high table," a British institution that is a fading relic of Commonwealth ties.

It was during an afternoon tea break that my silence finally ended. An athletic-looking fellow was trying to elicit interest in a softball game. I could barely contain myself. "Hey, you! I'd love to play." Heads turned as half the people in the room wondered where I had found my tongue. In no time my competitive zeal was displayed. I helped to organize a league, explained the rules, and, not coincidentally, became the main interpreter of the rules. If any single fact underscored the difference between the Aussies and myself, it was a softball game.

Like Etonians, these men came dressed in whites. They didn't pitch, they bowled. And if, perchance, one of their "mites" got a hit, they applauded politely and said "good shew." For an old stickball player, the proprieties were odd and annoying. I screamed at the opposing pitcher, cursed when someone on my team made an error, and came close to punching the umpire in a dispute over a bad call. I was a complete enigma to the Australians, a curiosity that was at once brash and resourceful. It seemed extremely odd that this normally laconic American should get so worked up over a modified cricket game.

My habits were undoubtedly strange, but I found Aus-

67

tralian post-game habits very natural—excessively natural. A beer after a long afternoon at play is often what
a sport is all about. But Aussies drink until taking another
sip without barfing becomes an excruciating ordeal. The
usual pub is, understandably, completely tiled, and looks
like a men's room with a podium. When someone does
vomit, which is not at all unusual, a barmaid gets a hose
and washes the wall down; for this service, she receives
about as much attention as someone who sneezes on a New
York subway platform.

It is a matter of pride that everyone have a chance to
"shout" (order and pay for the drinks) for everyone in the
group. If the group includes ten men, the number on a
softball team, ten pints of beer will be consumed in a
matter of two or three hours. After a session at the pub I
invariably crawled back to my room too sloshed to find
my bed, yet still sober enough to be amazed at the capacity
of the average Australian for beer. Generation after generation of males know the local pub better than their
homes. On many occasions I was told, "If a man can't
drink, he isn't worth knowing." Obviously, women are not
involved; the pub is an exclusive male preserve. Women
are relegated to the baby carriage run in a manner that
does not bespeak subtlety. On one occasion a friend had
sat in the pub for ten hours when his concerned wife sheepishly came by to inquire about his welfare. Her appearance led to so much laughter that the bloke couldn't show
his face again for months. He also refused to speak to his
wife for an equal period of time. It came as no surprise to
me to discover that Germaine Greer is an Australian.

The drinking habit is not restricted to certain segments
of the population. In fact, in a nation that prides itself on
an egalitarian spirit, everyone indulges himself with the

brew. One morning I had an appointment to see the leader of the Opposition Party in the House of Representatives. It was 10:00 A.M., but this gentleman—a W. C. Fields look-alike—was already putting away glasses of Johnnie Walker Black Label. When I inquired about his country's immigration policy, he burped and said, "Damn good." I wasn't sure whether he was referring to the booze or the policy. On another occasion I invited a representative to dinner at the dormitory, a fellow who had been in the House for twenty-eight consecutive years. It was the only meal I have ever drunk in my life. We started with sherry, had claret between mouthfuls of steak, had cognac after dinner, and finished with some serious beer drinking. I found that my modest stipend barely covered my liquor bills. I also discovered that even when these meals were arranged for research purposes, I could never recall what was said.

It is no wonder that Aussies like the easy life: they're too stoned to be energetic. There isn't a storekeeper in Canberra who isn't Italian or Greek; if the natives keep it up, recent immigrants may well acquire an iron grip on the country's retail establishments.

Australia is a middle-class paradise. No one works too hard, everyone owns a television set, and more than half the population is home on Saturday night watching *The Dean Martin Show*. The other half is watching Carol Burnett. Department stores have garments and products that resemble vintage Mays' sales. There is no variation in price; every suit costs $50. An Orchard Street brand or a Lord and Taylor's design is simply not available. About the only variation in price can be found in a pub—you can buy your beer in fifteen or sixty cent containers. Everyone drives a car; the favorite among the academic and youth set is the Mini-Minor, which is about half the size of a Volkswagen and comes with a free shoe horn. There is no racial strife; Australians are fond of telling Americans that Australia will never experience a Watts riot. Though a black-power movement was organized by Aborigines, it is unlikely that this indigenous population will rouse the Australians from their sweet somnolence. And if the Abos don't, no one else will.

Life for the Australian academic can be absolutely idyllic. There is simply no pressure: the "publish or perish" chant has not yet reached their shores. Aside from a weekly seminar, academics at the Australian National University could only be seen in the tea room. Presumably, they were busily at work on research that would expand the frontiers of knowledge. On occasion, though, I spied these alleged researchers snoozing behind open newspapers. The combination of free time, little pressure, and surroundings that would make the Palm Springs set envious does not inspire industry. With my New York orientation, pressure was self-imposed; I stood out like a rate-buster in a construction union.

As one might expect, discussions of Australian policies were on the scheduled agenda at the infrequent seminars that constituted the only noticeable pressure on the resident academics. Invariably, the exchanges seemed to center upon Vietnam—the sole preoccupation of almost everyone in 1967—even among otherwise complacent Australian professors. Having been an anti-war advocate since 1963—when my regular reading of I. F. Stone began—these discussions were usually interesting, so interesting, in fact, that I was probably the only American of my age to be converted from an anti-war advocate to an equivocal pro-war defender in the period from 1965 to 1967. I continued to equivocate because, as a New York liberal, I just couldn't be pro-war, even while imbibing Max Ascoli in large doses. Australians can present a very convincing case for balance-of-power theories that, to most Americans, seem like the scribbles on Herman Kahn's blackboard. Australia almost went to war with Indonesia in the early sixties, and the people still possess vivid recollections of the Japanese invasion of Darwin in 1942. It is interesting to note, too, that the distance between Darwin and Saigon is less than the distance between Sydney and Darwin, a fact that was used as a justification for Australia's interest in Asian affairs. Some might even term this a paranoid interest in Asian affairs. Nonetheless, from an early sixties perspective it became easier for me to understand why former Prime Minister Robert Menzies could prevail upon the United States to get involved in Southeast Asia through the SEATO Treaty. Australia was hardly one of those dominoes discussed at length by Dulles and Eisenhower, but it had good historical reasons for fearing the worst. For narrow-minded peaceniks of the sixties, only "presentism" served as a guide for policy decisions. Having been a former peacenik, I understood the syndrome; moreover, I also came to understand what foreign policy position the United States had been trying to evolve.

It must seem strange that a kid from Brooklyn would be moving directly against the historical current. But American power can appear quite different when viewed from a relatively weak state possessing modest defense capabilities. Like Pete Hamill, I schizophrenically longed for "radical chic" and *machismo* together. Some might even argue that *macho* was dominant in my particular case; but I think that my Australian experience allowed me to acquire a viewpoint other than the one imbibed at weekly incestuous anti-war meetings. Having been taught a foreign policy view predicated on an aversion to Dulles's brinkmanship and Robert Taft's isolationism, it wasn't too difficult for me to accept the idea of America's international role in a "conventional war." What *was* difficult, however, was retaining my liberal credentials when all of my so-called liberal friends were making sounds that were unmistakably Taft-like.

Australians rationalize their foreign policy about as well as Americans for Democratic Action or Young Americans for Freedom. Certain key phrases have been learned pat by even the most naive observers: "N.P.T." (nuclear proliferation treaty), regional defense network, Anzus, Aspac, and a host of other acronyms have entered the lexicon of common usage. The left in Australia acts as if history stopped in the thirties. Its rhetoric is based on orthodox class warfare, even while its adherents reap the benefits of the middle-class cornucopia. A left-wing infatuation with regional brotherhood and mutual friendship has about as much utility at the moment as would placing love beads on Arab and Israeli leaders in an effort to end their mutual hatred. But the left was a hopeless minority group until Nixon, of all people, gave it a renewed vitality through his overtures to China. Yet even the Labor victory in the 1972 national election probably did not change the fundamentally complacent character of the nation.

Australians, regardless of who leads them, will demand leisure time, time to get out "in the bush for a barb" (barbecue). Everyone seems to adore the out-of-doors. When they are not watching tele, they are picnicking, playing tennis, driving cross-country, or hiking. Cultural refinements, except for a few centers located in Sydney and Adelaide, are virtually nonexistent. Interestingly, I think,

72

Americans pride themselves on local museums yet rarely attend them, preferring instead to remain home and watch the Sunday football game. Australians, on the other hand, lament the lack of cultural activity, but can be found camping out along the Murray or the Murrinbidgee River, or actively participating in some event. Of course, this crude generalization reflects my limited view and does not reflect the changing times. There are now so many campers at Big Sur that there is a policy of standing room only. And the traditional Australian Rules championship game will attract a hundred thousand spectators and several million viewers. Nonetheless, I hold fast to my original distinction.

What this analysis suggests is that the America one sees from the other side of the world is neither so evil nor so desirable as critics and chauvinists would have us believe. Notwithstanding the view of Susan Sontag, the world would not be better off if America incinerated itself. While left-wing critics deride our culture as patently vapid, Australians wait patiently for hours to see a revival of *Gone with the Wind*. While anti-war critics denounced American participation in "an unnecessary and shameful war," there were people in the South Pacific who genuinely appreciated our war efforts. While the American left castigates the lower middle class as "pigs," these "pigs" are eminently more sophisticated and refined than the average Aussie one meets in a pub. While William Whyte and others decry the national tendency toward conformity, this land still offers more options for self-expression than presently exist in Australia.

Likewise, when the American Chamber of Commerce describes the nation as active, it neglects the sedentary character of corporate occupations and suburban living.

When Birchers uphold the national honor, they do not consider the blatant value schisms that eat away at our guts
like cancer cells. When our leaders tell us to see America's
scenic beauties first, they ignore the ugliness wrought by
industrial waste.

Admittedly, you can't have natural beauty *and* wide-
spread industrialization; they cannot coexist and Australians recognize that intuitively. They have opted to
preserve the pristine qualities of the land, although their
struggle against industrial despoliation is far from over.
Americans have viewed—and, to a great extent, still view
—their wildernesses as areas to be harnessed and con-
quered. Our tradition is Las Vegas and Miami, not Grand
Teton Park. The cement mixer was regarded, not as a
hazard, but as a manifestation of destiny. Contrast this
attitude with the national resistance to further development
of the Australian "Gold Coast." When the plan was first
proposed, Sydney *Morning Herald* editorials noted, "Australia doesn't need a Miami Beach."

Despite the stark beauty of the land and my growing
fondness for many Aussies, I couldn't wait to leave the
country after my one year there. Australian provincialism
was just too heavy after Greenwich Village. I'll never forget the time I went to see Mai Zetterling's *Night Games* in
Melbourne, only to sit through a thirty-five-minute version
of the two-hour film that had been thoroughly sliced and
spliced by the state censor. Similarly, when I ordered
books from abroad, I received a note instructing me to
pick them up at a customs office, a rather unusual practice.
When I inquired about my property, the customs officer
asked if I were importing lewd literature for public distribution. You see, among the books I had ordered was a

74

copy of Alain Resnais's screenplay for *Hiroshima Mon Amour*; the book included film stills, one of which showed a nude couple in bed. In the mind of this supernumerary, I was a pervert looking at pictures rightfully banned from Australia.

It is also true that I missed being in America. There is nothing in Australia that can duplicate the smells of MacDougal Street. Even Australian hippies appeared unauthentic to me, like some kind of rip-off for public voyeurism. Australia's efforts to imitate American products or customs usually came off poorly. America's future will undeniably affect the policies of other nations: its problems will, in all probability, reappear elsewhere; its successes, often deemed problems in other lands, are likely to be merchandized abroad before the first television commercial announcing their arrival has been completed. In Australia, anything characterized as American, no matter how inane, is usually greatly appreciated. A Midwest-terner who claimed never to have been "curried below the knees" used to take his leave from the Australian National University tearoom by bellowing, "See you round the doughnut." I thought the remark was about as humorous as Richard Nixon telling his grandfather's favorite story. Yet every time he said it—and that was at least twice a day —the Aussie academics roared in appreciation. "Now *that's* a genuine Americanism," they would say; I pretended I didn't hear them.

Australian values can often be as empty or as uplifting as the American variety. Both nations value materialism and both admire their frontier heroes, except that ours is named Billy the Kid and theirs Ned Kelly. They also share a Horatio Alger tradition and a spirit of "fair play." Yet it is the United States that remains the unpredictable factor, the state upon whose destiny continents like Australia depend.

I know that it's fashionable among certain Americans to be anti-American. Every once in a while (at the subway stop around 5:30 P.M., for example), even an I.C. type like myself hates this nation; but from what I've seen, the action is all here. This isn't the most relaxing land, nor is it the best place to raise kids or the nation with the best schools, but it does have the best knishes, the best pizza, the best basketball players, the best filmmakers, and the best artists: and if you want a sauna equipped with push-button, remote-control, temperature regulated ultraviolet rays that can be installed in minutes, where else in the world can you go? There isn't a single Hammacher Schlemmer in Australia.

As an intergenerational freak, I don't see all other places as inferior or superior to America. For my parents' generation, every time one set foot outside the nation one was assured of getting dysentery or worse. For the turned-on set, every trip to Europe or Asia is the millennium. One of my students told me that the real attraction in Europe are the rows of freshly baked bread displayed in local bakeries. Yet all I could think of was fly-infested bread ritually fingered by every passerby. I recall the story included in *Race and Nationality in American Life* about the Italian immigrant who continually told all his American friends how wonderful it was in the old country. After years of saving, he finally had enough money to return to Italy. But it wasn't the Italy he had expected. In fact, it didn't compare with the America he had been criticizing all these years. The author of the book, Oscar Handlin, concluded that this story, which has been retold in many second-generation homes, is like the one about the young man who gets married and, for the first time in his life, comes to appreciate his mother.

Australia had a similar effect on me. I never raised the black flag of anarchy or shouted "Tear it down," but I was very critical of America. To some extent, I still am. But that year abroad gave me a new perspective. I'm not ready to go to work for the Chamber of Commerce; yet I now realize that there is something magical about this country. I may still take many things here for granted, and at times I do feel like tearing this nation down, but that feeling is certainly less frequent since my voyage Down Under.

CHAPTER 6

Underground Notes from a Campus Ombudsman

WITHOUT HAVING THE SLIGHTEST IDEA as to what I might do when I returned from Australia, I called the only academics I knew and asked for a job. Convinced as they were that I had been doing something significant in an exotic land, these former teachers and soon-to-be colleagues hired me as an assistant professor. For the first time in ten years, or since I was known as *the* basketball player, I had an identity. Now my parents could say "My son, the professor." Of course, they preferred to say "My son, the doctor," and I did have a Ph.D. to confuse the issue.

Being a professor, however, was not the only role I sought. In my desire to confront the times, to test my ideological predilections against reality, I wanted to do something else. I didn't have to wait too long to find out what that would be.

At a time when students and faculty were complaining about everything, there had to be someone, I thought, who could mediate between opposing groups. It was a rational assumption based upon irrational conditions. And like other rational assumptions, I adopted its implications as if it were a demonstrated truth.

Having been convinced by Hannah Arendt that large bureaucratic institutions (like the one that employs me) are often insensitive to student grievances, I was already predisposed to the idea of a campus ombudsman before the matter ever came up. From personal experience I felt reasonably sure that thoughtless bureaucratic decisions were usually not the fault of administrators—who, on the whole, are about as thoughtful as the faculties from which they come—but of a spiraling bureaucratization process that disperses responsibility and decision-making until it becomes impossible to determine how decisions were made and who is responsible for enforcing them. An ombudsman could cut red tape, or so I thought, if he were given a free hand in representing aggrieved students. Ideally, he could locate and remedy flaws in the bureaucratic system.

At the end of the academic year, several student leaders approached me about the possibility of being nominated for the position of ombudsman. (Students were permitted one nomination, the faculty three). Since I had been out of the country for some time, and had cautiously guarded my anonymity upon returning to the university, I thought my nomination resulted more from my age (I was under thirty at the time) than from any special qualifications which I may have possessed for the role. I accepted the nomination, thinking that my anonymity militated against my election. And I was correct.

Losing the election was a disappointment, since I secretly coveted the role more than I admitted. On the other hand, I could rationalize the loss by daydreaming about an ombudsman drowning in a sea of paper work. Both these hopes and fears were reawakened when the victor unexpectedly resigned from the position one month after he had been elected. A special run-off of the remaining candidates was conducted. This time no rationalization or disappointment was forthcoming. I was elected by the narrowest of margins and was now the campus ombudsman.

No trumpets blared as I entered my office the following day. In fact, there was no change in my life at all for several days, aside from a few congratulatory messages and some snide comments. Not one student had come to complain. When the vice-dean called to "negotiate" (his word) my released time for "my new responsibilities," I could not argue very forcefully for much more than one third of my university commitment (which was less than the recommendation made by the representative student organizations) since, for all practical purposes, I did not have a new job.

This all changed more quickly than I care to remember. Seven months later I was still recovering from the "ombudsman bends," an occupational hazard I'd discovered. My exposure to my constituents began when the editor of the *Graduate Students' Organization Newsletter* wrote an article about my personal background and the responsibilities connected with my job. From some very undisciplined reading about the Scandinavian and New Zealand ombudsmen, I had a vague idea of the role, but the article was my first real exposure to the duties of a campus ombudsman. In bold print I read that the ombudsman shall be authorized to "examine any complaint brought to him by a student or a group of students of his college" and "call for a review of any decision of any

official or committee, or of the faculty, that is related to
the complaint, and to appeal to a higher authority when
the possibility exists; but he shall not be authorized to
alter said decision by his own action alone." How this
directive would relate to my actual functions I couldn't
predict, but the publication of the article and the subsequent arrival of complainants gave me a chance to find out.

Being compulsively conscientious about my new position, I was determined to find out what other ombudsmen
had done so that I would then be in a better position to
decide what I should do, rather than rely upon trial and
error. The literature revealed that the role was a mixed
bag. Some ombudsmen were merely another arm of the
administration and were branded by student militants as
"a tool of the establishment." Others were initiators of student activism, using the role as a soapbox for SDS-style
rhetoric. There were also some ombudsmen with a keenly
developed sense of morality: they viewed the position as
the university's conscience and proceeded to act like clois-
tered Benedictines.

After an examination of the literature, I was more convinced than ever that I was conspicuously unqualified for
the role: I am not, nor have I ever been, diplomatic in my
relations with colleagues—an indispensable requirement
of an ombudsman. My institutional commitment is directly related to the courses I am permitted to teach, to
administrative cooperation with my research projects, to
financial assistance, to released time, and to salary incre-
ments. My concern for students is related to their willingness to use rational and thoughtful processes for the solution of problems, quite an anachronistic notion at this
time. I am not particularly tolerant of students who, lacking real grievances, present only those they have been able

81

to fabricate. In referring to the specific role criteria cited by various groups on the campus, I could cite all of the following as legitimate excuses: lack of familiarity with the operation and regulations of the school; a philosophical gap when dealing with the more activist students; a lack of authority partially resulting from my anonymity among most of my colleagues; and an ineffectiveness in handling administrative matters, attributable to inexperience.

Clearly recognizing my unpreparedness for the post, I was still eager to handle my first case. As it turned out, it was more eventful than I had anticipated. An elderly woman in her sixties led a moderately attractive young lady into my office and introduced herself as the complainant's mother. While she proceeded to explain the details of the alleged grievance, her daughter sat silently and stared at my maps of the world. For one hour I listened to the mother rant on about the unfairness existing in the school and the young professors who were jealous of her daughter's ability. But I was unable to discern a problem until the daughter finally interrupted her mother and said, "What my mother has neglected to say is that the chairman won't permit me to serve in the guidance program." The words "guidance program" almost blew my mind. This young girl, obviously still entangled in her mother's apron strings, wanted to counsel others! Making a conscious effort to avoid prejudicial statements, I addressed my questions to the girl; she seemed less objectionable than her garrulous mother. However, every question was inevitably answered by mom. "What qualifications do you have to pursue a graduate degree in that department?" I asked. "Why, professor, don't you know that my daughter is a member of Mensa?" All I could say was, "Congratulations. I think you deserve each other." While ushering them out under the continuous pressure of my right arm, I promised to investigate the matter further.

The very next day I called an adviser in the guidance program for an appointment. After mentioning my name several times (to no avail), I yielded to impulse and said, "The ombudsman is calling." My appointment was scheduled for that afternoon.

As I had suspected, most of the department's professors agreed that the young lady's academic performance was satisfactory but doubted that she possessed the maturity to be an adequate baby-sitter. In an effort to be fair, one professor remarked, "Let her reapply when she shows signs of growing up."

Despite my displeasure, I decided to call the young lady to tell her that she might reapply in "a semester or two"— I wasn't sure how long it would take to "grow up." As luck would have it, her mother answered the phone; before I could even deliver my message, she notified me that her daughter had left for Europe "to work things out and find herself." Case closed—at least temporarily.

Just as I hung up the receiver, my secretary informed me, "A very angry woman is here to see the ombudsman." For reasons I am unable to explain, everyone I knew referred to me in the third person; and I replied the same way. "Tell her the ombudsman will see her in five minutes."

Once again a middle-aged woman came into the office. I was beginning to think I had a strange attraction for mothers. Before I could introduce myself, she raged, "I've never suffered such indignities in my life. I must have satisfaction." "What happened?" I asked meekly, fearful that her flailing arms might hit me in the stomach. "You'll never believe this. I've been attending this university for several years and have never been treated so discourteously. A professor at least ten years my junior had the nerve to refer to me as Sadie instead of Mrs. Perlman." I feigned serious concern about the charge, promised immediate satisfaction, ushered her out the door, and shook my head in despair.

When I told a member of the administration about these cases, he said, "The crazy ones have a new office to bring their complaints to." It was obvious the kooks were coming, but I wasn't sure whether I was coming or going. In my feeble effort to describe my duties to a colleague, I wrote the following note, which was later affixed to my office door:

> He hears about your woe, investigates
> your problem, and finds a magic remedy.
> He is your counsel, friend, confidante.
> Please don't be disturbed by the
> thunder you hear in his presence.

One of my students added this inscription to the sign: "Is he a shrink, the fuzz, or Underdog? No! He's Ombatman!" After my experience with the next grievant, I was fairly certain that some students mistakenly regarded me as a "shrink."

A plain-looking girl with very thick glasses and stains all over her blouse requested some advice from the ombudsman. She wanted to know whether it was appropriate for a student to give a professor a gift. This hardly seemed a matter that I should be concerned with, but her urgency made me attentive. "Why are you seeking advice from me?" I asked. "Surely it would be advisable to discuss this with your professor." For an extended minute she just stared into space; finally she said, "I really wanted to get your impression of the gift." She slipped a white card out of a carrying case and showed it to me. The card was constructed like a triptych, with each section having what seemed to be a globe and a fetus. "What is the significance of the drawing?" I innocently inquired. "Significance? Significance?" she replied, the words becoming increasingly more faint. Again she stared out blankly into space, in what I considered a catatonic trance. No other words were uttered; after several minutes she left without as much as a farewell. As soon as she had departed, I called a university psychiatrist and described the incident. He contacted her, scheduled several interviews, and placed her in his care; two months later I learned from the clinic that the young lady was under "intensive care" and had made "a dramatic improvement."

I was soon to learn that most student grievances were of a very different kind. Some required the same length of time it takes to process a transcript; others were concerned with refunds which the university had neglected to process; still others dealt with the lack of a sufficient number of security police to cope with the increasing violence encountered by evening students. For several weeks I was clerk, secretary, bursar, and security policeman. I spent as much time in the recording office as I did in my classes. To my surprise, the expenditure of time led to positive results: I soon realized that the real "bureaucratic problem" at the university was the surly clerk who remained unconcerned about even the most legitimate student requests. This unseen and relatively anonymous individual (usually a single girl attentive only to the more handsome male graduate students) is the real scourge of the university. She possesses virtually unlimited power over students and, more important, is usually not supervised by administrators. For all practical purposes, she has as much of a say as to whether or not a student will graduate as any faculty member, and, from my own observation, is accorded more respect by students.

The kind of case I relished dealt with the quality of teaching and course offerings. If there is one thing an ombudsman should be concerned with, it is the presumed university goal of educating its students. When this did not occur satisfactorily, I was prepared to jump into the nearest telephone booth, change into my work clothes, and fly into action.

As a consequence of my job, I soon discovered which colleagues prepare for class sessions, attend class, are inebriated in class, are indiscreet with students, or try to seduce every sweet thing in a mini-skirt. It was just the kind of data needed for a new Edward Albee play, but, with the exception of a few comments to my wife, I didn't break the faith.

Several students holding fellowships arrived in my office to complain about A's. This was certainly a new one on me. In a "special program" (you can always tell a special program by the large number of complaints) designed for these students, they were asked to take a semester of independent study in which specially tailored projects were pursued. However, these students claimed that they had no supervision, requirements, papers, conferences, seminars, or anything else. They were just "given a vacation"—as they put it—and rewarded with A's.

Another student with a grade problem described a formula his professor had devised to determine grades (the very fact that a "formula" existed made me sympathetic to the student). The only problem was that his grade at the end of the semester was lower than his accumulated average. I called the professor and was told that in the middle of the semester he had decided to change the formula without informing the class of the revision. When I diplomatically suggested that this oversight might have penalized some students, he said, "who the hell are you to interfere with my academic freedom?" Case closed. It was obvious that a few professors used academic freedom as an excuse for almost any ill-advised action.

Still another student told me of a class in which the professor, without informing the class or providing for a substitute, missed the first four sessions. The student demanded a refund, a request that was quite unprecedented, but seemingly justified. In order to avoid the embarrassing situation of holding a hearing for a tenured faculty member, the administration refunded the tuition.

The issue of race has generated considerable anxiety at almost every reputable university. Things have been fairly cool at my school, a fact which may be attributable to an unworthy university, fairness, a docile student body, the lack of controversy, or a sensitive faculty. I've attributed the condition to the faculty. As a faculty member who can easily be placed in the middle of a confrontation, I've been particularly sensitive about the issue. Perhaps that explains why I was solicitous about the first charge of racism directed at a faculty member. Mr. Gomez, a Puerto Rican student, reported "racist conditions" in a Spanish class "so humiliating" that he could not "perform as expected." He provided little evidence to substantiate this serious charge except a disagreement over dialect, which hardly constituted signs of racism, and a grade of D, which the student argued was unwarranted. The episode that follows clearly points up the problem often faced by a faculty member who is "color blind."

According to the records, Mr. Gomez received a numerical grade of 33 on the final exam, which, the professor noted, accounted for two thirds of his grade. Since Mr. Gomez attained a C average on other papers and quizzes, the final grade seemed fair. The professor admitted that the average gave no indication of the grade on any one test. I therefore felt obliged to let a friend examine the final exam paper; he thought the grade was generous. What I did not know at the time was why Gomez had challenged the grade. At a later meeting he noted that his view of the incident had been affected by the grade he received in a graduate linguistics course. In that class he scored an 11 on the final and did poorly in his class work; by every indication he deserved to fail, yet he received a C as a final grade. When questioned about this, the linguistics professor admitted quite candidly, "I wanted to avoid charges of racial discrimination and maintain good ties with the Puerto Rican community. Sure he deserved to fail, but no harm will come of the C."

When I told Mr. Gomez that his charges were unfounded, he screamed, "This is an insult to my name, my family, my people, and my nation." I have not heard from him since.

The most unforgettable student I met during my term in office was poor Mr. Chang (the "poor" is not a sign of condescension). This student had been in and out of every administrative office at the university; he spoke to any receptive listener and would go on interminably recounting his tale of woe. He was one of the most charming and articulate students I've met, and if the paintings he showed me are any indication, he may also have been among the most talented.

Mr. Chang came to see me about the "incomplete" grade he had received in an art history class. According

88

to his account, he was asked to do a "special project" in his area of expertise—Chinese silk-screen painting— which was tantamount to writing a scholarly book. Since he was unable to complete the project by the end of the semester, he did not challenge the grade. What complicated matters, though, was the fact that his inability to complete the project the following semester would mean that the incomplete grade would automatically become a failure; in addition, he would lose his state scholarship (and would thus be unable to offer financial assistance to his ailing mother in Hong Kong), he would jeopardize his standing in the department, and the time needed to earn his degree would be prolonged. Now you can understand why he was "poor" Mr. Chang. Every day posed another threat for him. On one occasion his typewriter broke down, thus preventing him from further work on his project; on another, the bundle of notes which he carried everywhere was swept up in a gust of wind.

To remain insensitive to his plight was impossible, I thought. I soon found out differently. Clerks detested him because he invariably registered late for courses, a sin long remembered by girls who were obliged to leave their offices five minutes later than usual. Mr. Chang was busy selling his canvasses up until the last moment of registration. The fact that he was forced to do this as a result of his poverty was conveniently forgotten by those concerned. Several administrators said that he was "a nuisance, always hanging around the place." Sure he was; but no one paid any attention to him anyway. A faculty member remarked, "Oh, Chang. He can bring tears to anyone's eyes; that's how he gets away with murder." I was unable to determine whose murder he was getting away with.

Chang's professor denied that he had asked him to write

a book. "All I wanted," he insisted, "was an outline." Chang presented a note written by the professor indicating that the contrary was true. In addition, Chang argued that he had already completed several chapters of the book which he felt could be substituted for term papers. However, "a congenital Oriental self-effacement" (his term) prevented him from meeting with the professor or letting him read the chapters. Pride and "professorial authority" were reasons the professor gave for being firm. As I saw it, the only way to cut the Gordian knot was to negotiate a compromise that might offend the professor, yet not alienate him completely. I asked the chairman whether Chang could use his completed chapters to eliminate the incomplete and finish his project as "independent study," while still maintaining his matriculation in the department. He agreed, even though the professor bitterly reproved the action.

Mr. Chang still registers late, I've been told, and is still castigated by clerks; but he doesn't care as much anymore. He contends that he has a special friend who looks out for him. I treasure that friendship.

Not all of the cases had such happy endings. Several weeks after the Chang affair, a girl with a voice reminiscent of Marilyn Monroe requested a "very private talk" with the ombudsman. She "complained" (I don't think the term accurately describes her problem) that one of her professors was trying to seduce her. A basic shyness, I guess, prevented me from asking probing questions. I said, "What evidence do you have?" "Well," she hesitated for a moment, "he has asked me out to lunch. And even though we weren't alone, he *did* stare at me. And those eyes; he has this way of looking at me . . ." When I foolishly asked her to describe the look, she proceeded to contort every muscle in her face. It was perfectly obvious to me, at any rate, that this girl was projecting and imposing her fantasies on her most recent captive audience. I did not doubt that seductions occurred with ever-increasing frequency at the school, but I felt positive that no one was seducing this chick. Losing my cool for a minute, I said, "If you have no better evidence than a look, I suggest that you find some." She did not waste any time leaving my office. I've discovered that tact is not always my bag. I've also discovered that I have unwittingly been co-opted by those under thirty in one significant way: the student vernacular is now partially my own. I don't feel any more hip, but I sound it.

Nonetheless, I am certainly not what you would call an unequivocal defender of student rights, nor am I unsympathetic to many student complaints. My one year as an ombudsman convinced me that academics, like any other group, can be insensitive—and so can students. Needless to say, both groups have redeeming qualities; it just seemed that I was always dealing with those who had few, if any, positive traits. Like most activities in which a product of I.C. engages, I am caught, caught between those who want instant reform and those who will resist it at all costs. Perhaps my relative success, if I can call it that, stemmed from the fact that I didn't have a hard line. It's also true that an ombudsman who fails to adopt a firm position on either side of the argument can become a target for both parties. I've discovered that if I agree to act as a target, the mutual enmity that proponents and antagonists direct toward me may allow them to reach temporary, perhaps even enduring, understandings. With this in mind, it would probably be accurate to describe my role as ombudsman as that of a dart-board, there for the mutual satisfaction that results from ventilating one's hostility in socially acceptable channels. Unfortunately, a dart-board has no one who will hear its complaints.

My I.C. also made me philosophical about most grievances—infuriatingly so for student reformers. I was sure student representation on every university committee wouldn't bring instant justice, just as I am convinced that faculty committees do little more than allow professors time to discuss their gripes. The world will not be a better place because we have ombudsmen, a truth known by every I.C. product who is skeptical of panaceas. Unfortunately, there are a lot of people without I.C. who grasp at straws; there are also mountebanks who exaggerate claims for the latest social solution in order to advance their own careers.

CHAPTER 7

1970 in Microcosm: A View from the Barricades

IT WAS THE YEAR OF THE STRIKE. Kent State. Cambodian Invasion. The words need no description for the media progeny. As a product of I.C., I didn't quite know what to make of all the furor. I looked on in disbelief, and even mock anger, as hordes of people marched and clenched fists shot into the air. I found myself at the corner of Washington Square Park and Washington Place trying to listen to a speaker screaming through an overamplified mike. He was unintelligible, but that made no difference to those who were screaming their approval. A high school student standing next to me was even more enraged than the rest of the crowd. He yelled, "Tear it down!" "It" was not identified, of course. I said, "Excuse me, but what do you want to tear down?" He replied, "Everything, this nation." "And why," I continued, "are you so angry?" "Atrocities, man, atrocities!" Since the answers to my previous questions were so predictable, I decided to pursue a different tack. "Can you understand that speaker?" I inquired. He answered, "That schmuck isn't worth listening to." "Then why do you not only listen but scream in obvious approval?" I asked. "I don't know, he's running the show." "Why aren't *you* a leader? Surely you can do a better job." "Me?" he asked in disbelief, "Me? Why, I can't even grow a mustache."

For me, May, 1970, will always be remembered as mustache month. It wasn't that I treated events that were patently serious in a cavalier fashion. But in my eagerness to understand the feelings of the younger set, to get to the root of their problem, I encountered fair-haired youths who were preoccupied with growing mustaches. It was a time of symbols. Long hair, peace signs, flags, and hard-hats took on a special meaning at a time when nerve ends were exposed. I even found myself entrapped in defending a symbol.

Since I had been appointed to the faculty, I had remained conspicuously silent at faculty meetings. It wasn't that I had nothing to say; rather a combination of reserve and reticence to be described as a "hot shot" militated against my speaking up. Besides, I was always rather shy, and since the dean conducted faculty meetings in the manner of Stalin at the Supreme Soviet, I wasn't about to challenge his authority.

The day after the Kent State slaughter, meetings were held in universities across the country. At my college, a meeting was called to discuss what action faculty and students might take. In no time at all it degenerated into a rally, complete with raised arms and "right on!" shrieks eroding even the facade of decorum. I sat in disbelief as an aging professor walked up to the stage, wrestled the

94

microphone out of the hands of the faculty senator, and proceeded to deliver a one-hour monologue on the evils of American fascism that would have been an insult to the intelligence of John Steinbeck's Lenny. It wasn't a time for cool heads.

On May 11, 1970, the faculty council, of which I was a member, met to discuss what action we might recommend to the entire faculty. After considerable wrangling over the wording—I've never met two faculty members who could agree on anything quickly except salary increases—it was resolved that: *At their option* (my italics), students may be excused from classes and finals for the duration of the semester." Considering the sincere expressions of concern, it seemed only reasonable to accommodate anti-war activists, yet, at the same time, give those who wished to attend class the opportunity to exercise that right. I thought this seemed like a sensible proposal, and with the endorsement of the council it had an excellent chance of passing at the faculty meeting.

While students demonstrated at the front of the auditorium, the faculty met to discuss the motion. Despite a few guerilla-theater types who shouted "shut it down," on the whole the meeting went smoothly. Those who opposed the motion maintained that the severity of the recent incident warranted a symbolic action by the faculty in the form of a total strike. It was obviously a reasonable view for anyone who shared that position, but from my perspective it disregarded the rights of those who had paid for and wished to attend classes. Since I found myself the unwilling leader of a caucus that felt uneasy about presenting its view, I proceeded to prepare my first major address to the faculty. I felt like Cicero before the Roman Senate. The words flowed with all the pomposity one would expect from an academic. Despite my recognition of the other side's symbolic position, I neglected to recognize the symbolism in my own presentation. My throat was dry, I coughed several times before I spoke, but the thought of my role as a leader helped me to rise to the occasion.

Colleagues,

I have decided to read this speech rather than speak extemporaneously because I am sure that my present enraged state would not permit me to present my ideas coherently.

I would like to express my singular dismay with regard to what has been happening at our university this week. I too share the general sense of outrage at what has happened at Kent State. I too am mortified by Vice-President Agnew's incendiary remarks. I too am disquieted by Attorney General Mitchell's tactics. But I cannot understand how the self-appointed interpreters of morality can blatantly disregard the rights of those who disagree with them. Isn't a university a place where ideas are freely exchanged, where tolerance is part of the modus operandi, *and where personal idiosyncrasies do not appear openly as mindless assaults?*

Is the Marcusean logic that legitimates "polymorphous perversity" and incivility to be accepted by institutions of learning? Is the search for truth to be sacrificed to the existential feeling that is associated with roaming the streets?

Perhaps academic freedom is an antediluvian notion to be discarded with the first student demand. Perhaps "winning" is more important than thinking. Perhaps the catharsis that results from involvement is more significant than weighing the evidence. If so, I suggest that this faculty endorse the actions of the new S.S. I suggest that we take over meetings and I suggest,—excuse me, demand—that we forcibly prevent rational disagreement.

If, however, you wish to preserve what is left of this institution, then consider the passage of the motion to permit this school to remain open. Let those who want to strike be protected from academic disqualificaion. But don't let this school, or any school, get involved in subscribing to political movements. Isn't this just a kind of inverted McCarthyism? Whether you agree with the

*prevailing sentiment or not is irrelevant; I am urging you to pro-
tect yourselves. Strike if you feel a sense of moral indignation, but
preserve the right of a university to remain free of coercion.*

There was modest applause, but I felt satisfied, purged
of my indignation. In the vote that followed, the faculty
approved the motion by a vote of 120 to 103. This meant
that the school would remain open, but demonstrators
would have the right to be absent without penalty. However, as an olive branch to the minority, another motion
was proposed and approved:

Be is resolved that the faculty go on record as opposing the
military action in Southeast Asia, and that we recommend an
immediate and unconditional withdrawal of all United States military forces from that area.

It seemed to me that the motion had as much meaning as
my signing a petition to end air pollution in New York.
Interestingly, the dean was so eager to appease this anti-
war position that he took no hand vote on the issue, even
though the voiced "nays" were almost as loud as the
"yeas." At that point I was emotionally enervated, but I
took comfort in what I thought was the end of a very
uncomfortable period.

Actually, it was just the beginning. When the University Senate, representing all the constituent colleges, met
to discuss the matter, it was noted that *only* one college
would remain open. To my surprise and the dean's dismay,
every other college faculty had decided to close its doors.

The very next day an unexpected and hastily called faculty meeting was organized. The dean disingenuously said
that he had decided to reconvene the faculty after consulting
with several students who had requested another vote, as
well as with several faculty who had misunderstood the
vote. He also asked that another motion be considered to

"suspend the formal operation of all courses for the remainder of the semester." Obviously, this was a palpable contradiction of the decision taken the previous day; it was also a violation of *Robert's Rules* and, from my point of view, showed a total disregard for faculty decisions. One faculty member asked the dean, "Do we continue to vote until we do it correctly?" Undeterred, the dean sought endorsement. Another faculty member, convinced that students, no matter how naive, represent the forces of light and goodness, said, "If we don't have the moral conviction to lead our students, the least we can do is to follow them." The applause was thunderous, but I just scratched my head trying to make sense out of that *non-sequitur*. Then a student asked for permission to speak. Amid sobs that reminded me of Mary Astor in the final scene of *The Maltese Falcon*, this girl employed every turgid device in her bag of wiles to convince us that if the college were not closed her generation would be demoralized, she would have no valid reason for attending college, she would likely turn to drugs, and there was just no telling what her enraged friends would do to our cherished buildings. How could one resist this appeal? It was a combination of gloom, threats, and the moral demise of a sweet nineteen-year-old. When the vote was taken, the faculty reversed its previous decision and now supported the dean's motion by a vote of 220 to 3. So overwhelming was the about-face that I still wonder if that girl wasn't really Mary Astor in disguise.

I left the auditorium a little sick to my stomach. As I was departing I met the vice-dean, the only member of the deanery who had the guts to excoriate the faculty charade. All he said was, "I don't believe it. Some of those people are, indeed, politically naive, but . . . I just don't believe

98

it." I didn't believe it either, and the more I thought about it, the more I found it unacceptable. It wasn't that my symbolic position had been defeated by the vote; it was that the rules were violated. I was always willing to compete, always took my losses hard, but I never could understand changing the rules to suit someone's personal advantage. And that, it seemed to me, was what had happened.

At seven o'clock that evening, after putting aside my uneaten food, I decided to write a letter to each and every one of my students explaining the college's decision and my subsequent action. It was an impulsive act, but once again I felt as if there was only the alternative of keeping my mouth shut and suffering through a good many uneaten meals. I liked food too much for that. So I sent the letter by registered mail to twenty-three students at a cost of almost forty-seven dollars. I mention the cost because it is a crude but effective indication of my dedication at the time. Since I couldn't be deceitful, the deans also received a copy. The letter read:

May 12, 1970

Dear _____:

I have decided, despite the policy statement issued by the college faculty, to resume *formal* classes this Thursday, May 14, at the appropriate time and place. In addition, I will expect all term papers to be submitted at that time. If you can provide evidence of constructive protest activity, an "incomplete" will be given as a final grade. This grade will automatically become an "F" unless all work is submitted by the end of the next academic semester. If you lack such evidence and do not submit a paper, you will receive a grade of "F." Any complaints about this procedure should be directed to my office.

I am taking this stand to preserve what is left of my personal integrity. It seems to me that there is not much school integrity left. The right to disagree, to attend classes, has been ignored by a faculty resolution clearly designed to abrogate such rights. Anticipated student violence partially precipitated this move—a factor that warranted my symbolic action.

For those of you who do' come to class, we will engage in an extended discussion of the issues presently confronting this nation.

Sincerely,
Herb London

By the following morning the shit had really hit the proverbial fan. The dean called me to his office and suggested in no uncertain terms that I was "erratic, hotheaded, and emotionally unstable." His lieutenant, an associate dean, invited me to lunch to continue the tongue-lashing. Of course, I couldn't accept a lunch without offering something in return, so I prepared a rather vigorous defense of my position for the benefit of my host. It didn't go over too well; neither of us ate much lunch amid all the shouting. I found that the strike had a more desirable effect on my physique than the Stillman diet. On one point this dean was admittedly correct—well, partially correct: if your gripe is against the dean, he suggested, you should direct your verbal assault against him and not against the faculty. I did have a gripe against the faculty for its spineless decision, but I guess he was right in suggesting that the dean was the actual source of my hostility. So I wrote a petition in which I stated that "university administrators and the majority of the faculty have taken political stands as persons or as groups directly identifiable with New York University. *Such actions neither suit the functional purposes of academic institutions, nor are they advisable for preserving this university as an institution of higher learning. Are we now going to take a stand on every major political issue?*" (my italics) There was more to the petition, but this was its central argument. I

100

didn't have to wait very long to get an answer to what I thought was a rhetorical question.

At the next regularly scheduled faculty meeting (May 18, 1970), the following motion was introduced by the victorious anti-war legions: "The Faculty strongly recommends to the University Senate the modification of the university calendar to permit an intensive involvement of students and faculty in direct political activity preceding next November's general election." Anticipating just such a proposal, and eager for a chance to continue my vituperative barrage, I had prepared another short paper describing the events of the previous week and my interpretation of them. It read:

The purpose of my presentation is to examine a precedent that may affect future school policy. First, however, I think it necessary to comment on the establishment of that precedent.

On Monday, May 11, the Faculty Council met to consider the action the college might take with respect to its regular operation. Extended debate and compromise on the issues led to acceptance of the motion. Two representatives of the steering committee were present yet *did not* object to the unanimously carried motion. That afternoon the faculty was asked to vote on this motion. The issues, which may not have been clear at the earlier meeting, were being debated in detail when one professor unequivocally proposed that "classes and exams be cancelled." The amendment was defeated by a vote of 120 to 103; the original motion was passed by a large majority.

A meeting was then called without advance notification. We were asked to reconsider our earlier vote; several faculty members were apparently confused about their decision and students were "urgently requesting" that we reconsider our actions. Let me examine these reasons individually. Reason one suggests that "several" faculty members were confused about the previous day's vote. But can one establish whether "several" is more than 17 (the number of votes separating the two sides of the proposed amendment)? And even if, according to *Robert's Rules*, a new vote could be held, should the latter be conducted at an unpublicized meeting, without consideration of the previous day's resolution? If a new motion is in order, why were we informed that there was "no real difference" between the two? Reason two implies that "students" urgently requested us to consider our actions. But nowhere are these students named. If "face-saving" (not my phrase) is necessary, how can it be argued, as it was at the time, that we are not responding to pressure?

Let me offer the following analogy: after voting for a presidential candidate, I find that I mistakenly pulled the wrong lever. Several other voters indicate that they have made the same mistake and subsequently call for a new election to be held. Despite general surprise, a new, unannounced vote is conducted. Pressure from a lobbying group at the election booth forces the entire body politic to vote for a different slate of candidates whose positions are allegedly identical with those on the previous slate.

I wish to state my objection to the violation of democratic procedures evidenced at last week's meetings. There was an obvious difference between Monday's motion, which protected the rights of both those who wanted to attend classes and those who wanted to engage in anti-war protests, and Tuesday's, which tended to ignore the right of students to attend formal classes and the obligation of the university to hold them.

The university, as I see it, is designed to convey knowledge through classroom sessions. It is not a staging zone for anti-war protests. Your protests can be expressed through existing political channels and specialized lobby groups, but not within a university framework intended to protect the right to dissent. Your resolution calling for action in Southeast Asia was not even prefaced by the words "the large majority of faculty present at the meeting. . . ." You have thereby violated the freedom to dissent and have unwittingly helped to transform an institution of learning into an institution of moral judgment—with the loudest voices belonging to the moral interpreters.

Given the present climate of opinion, these developments come as no surprise. What I find absurd, however, is that *you*, the faculty, can do all this in the name of higher principles.

It is obviously too late to reverse the most recent decision to curtail academic activities; but I wish to point out to you as a group that future politically motivated actions and related attempts to disregard democratic procedures will so erode the legitimacy of the school that no euphemisms, however carefully couched, will be able to restore this quality.

Before I could finish, the booing began. It was certainly atypical of the faculty, but I guessed that they were getting a little tired of my lecturing. I know I was. There was another fact, a fillip, that I desperately wanted to mention, but my hostile reception and the dean's reddening face and pursed lips, convinced me to let it drop. I had in my hand a copy of *Robert's Rules* which stated that when an original motion is accepted, it, or substantially the same motion, can be considered at any future session. *"But in assemblies having regularly scheduled meetings, new motions can be raised only at regular sessions."* (my italics) A vote could have been taken if the faculty had decided, by a simple majority, to rescind the earlier decision. But this was not done, nor was the motion issue raised at a regularly scheduled meeting. I don't like nitpickers—and I was certainly becoming one—but in my effort to expose what I considered blatant bullying, I was perfectly prepared to use the small print to uphold my opinion.

There was one particularly satisfying moment that second week. When I sent that registered letter to my students in defiance of the school's action, I never expected more than a handful of people to show up. Yet everyone came; it was the first time all semester that I had one hundred percent attendance. If registered mail weren't so damn expensive, I might have considered those letters as a regular ploy. Even more impressive than the attendance was the attitude of the radicals in my class—they constituted well over a majority—who, while opposing my beliefs, vigorously supported my determination to stand up for them. It made me feel, for an instant at any rate, that my teaching wasn't all in vain. One radical student spokesman characterized this view when he wrote:

I actively participated in and am still working against the thinking and the causes shaping the attitudes that made the Cambodian invasion and the death of four humans a fact.

The courses I attended were meaningful courses in my development. I commend your decision to face the administration and students head-on and demonstrate that you stand behind the values you hold dear.

It was interesting that several faculty members (eleven to be exact) also sent me notes after the May 18th meeting, in which they concurred with the stand I had taken. This was very curious indeed, since only three faculty members had voted against the dean's resolution—and I had been one of them. One colleague who *did not* oppose the dean's motion wrote me the following note:

Thank you for the statement which you read at the faculty meeting last week. I feel deeply indebted to you for your illuminating and much-needed expression of your position, with which I concur.

If this proved anything, it demonstrated that the general impression of academics created by Edward Albee, among others, was even truer than the stereotype would tend to suggest. It also confirmed my previously held view that faculty members act like eunuchs and administrators like castrators.

In the long run my opinion did prevail. I guess this gave me about as much satisfaction as knowing that the Dodgers would ultimately prove their superiority despite the fact that the Giants had beaten them out for the 1951 pennant. A statement prepared by the University Senate the next fall noted:

It is our judgment that the university, like other communities and organizations in our society, has an inherent right to require the cooperation of its members in the performance of its educational functions, and to control and regulate the conduct and behavior of those members who tend to impede, obstruct, or threaten the maintenance of order and the achievement of the university's educational goals.

Regardless of the degree of sincerity displayed, no individual or group of individuals has the right to disrupt or interfere with the workings of the colleges, schools, and divisions of the university, or to halt the regular processes of education and service to its members. Regardless of moral impetus, no student or group of students has the right to deny the freedom of other members of the university community.

All I could think of when I saw these words was, "Where were you when I needed your assistance?"

That was truly a time of error and poor judgment. It was apparent to me that academia bore a strong resemblance to Elsinore. Professors just could not make decisions; when they did, it was at meetings hastily called, on poorly drafted motions, after debate unworthy of being called rational. In the end, all the talk about conscience and morality did not mean much when pitted against unmitigated student pressure.

When Tom Wolfe was asked to speak at a Vietnam War rally, after previous speakers had relied on every moral precept in their bag of selected passages from "The Sermon on the Mount," he observed that "moralisms are the foxholes for incompetents." He couldn't win any popularity contests against Allen Ginsberg with that line, but I, for one, found that the statement was right on the mark. With little or no consideration of the issues, university faculty and students across the land were willing to jeopardize two hundred years of tradition and precedent for the free exchange of ideas. It was like chopping down an old tree that had provided shade in order to make poles for anti-war placards. But this protest was inexcusable in an even more fundamental way. In the name of an absolute moral principle, every consideration for the welfare of others was disregarded. It seems patently extreme to compare these events with the rise of Nazism. Yet on one issue, noted by Peter Gay in *The Weimar Culture*, there does appear to be a similarity: as the need for absolute morality increases, the concern for human decency decreases.

Despite the impression created by many of my statements, I am not a purist. I did unwittingly adopt a rigid public stance; on reflection, I would probably do it again, although it wouldn't be easy. I like verbal combat, but I was using a pea-shooter against a battery of howitzers. I'm not trying to make myself the underdog, but I was becoming very unpopular; more important, I was marching directly into a hurricane called the *Zeitgeist*. There was a spirit of the times, a social and political force that, from my perspective, seemed inexorable in 1970. Sure, I exaggerated much that happened, just as my opponents envisioned apocalypse around the corner. That was part of the legacy of that month of May. The view from the barricades was one that reflected personal feelings at least as often as it did a dispassionate view of reality.

As a product of I.C., I was taught to withhold judgment until the evidence, or at least a share of it, could be exam-

106

ined. I believe in an exchange of views, even if I cannot muster Voltaire's optimism for the ultimate emergence of truth. I respect a university for its relative openness, recognizing, in an obvious gesture to Marcuse, that the university may sometimes be political, although it is not blatantly so. In an analogous manner I would argue that while an operating room, no matter how well scrubbed, still has germs, I would prefer to be operated on there than in a sewer. Similarly, I would prefer to be educated in an institution that has a fair degree of openness rather than in one that enforces the retention of an ideological catechism. In short, I was quite out of place among the demonstrators in May of 1970. What I was demonstrating for seemed to pale in significance when compared to the grandiose rhetoric of that year. But I wonder how many of the demonstrators remember the name of Cambodia's leader, or the length of time American troops stayed in Cambodia, or why Nixon claimed that an invasion was necessary? All this occurred only a few years ago, yet May 1970 has already been relegated to an attic of fading memories. That does not make me feel very comfortable at all.

In retrospect, my actions were rather atypical of views I have now espoused. But it is clear that even an I.C.'s faith in tolerance has its limits. Having been nurtured on the pure and undiluted decisions of Justice Black, I always assumed that others like myself wanted a free marketplace of ideas. However, while caught in the crunch, I recognized an emergent intolerance in my own views toward what I perceived as intolerance in the views of others. I was feeling a little like the demonstrators who used free speech placards to prevent Governor Wallace from speaking. Despite my suspicion of orthodoxies, it was obvious that I had been so enticed by my liberal assumptions that I didn't notice how greatly they had ossified. I.C., as a classification, is subject to the same problem: it often makes an orthodoxy out of rejecting orthodoxies. It is both a logical and emotional dilemma that surfaces when the times demand hard answers. It is also a refuge both for those unwilling to take a stand and for those who think that the issues are too complex to take an unalterable stand. To all who remember it, May 1970 was a very difficult month for I.C. types.

CHAPTER 8
Xanadu on the Hudson

THE MORE I THOUGHT ABOUT IT, the more irritated I became. It wasn't only the moralists who got to me; I knew what to expect from them. It was the weakness and inconsistency of what has been inaccurately described as a university "community." I knew that I needed a different kind of experience, one that was as far removed from the characteristic equivocation of academic life as summer camp is from boot camp.

In several articles which appeared in *Life* and *Time* magazines, I read about one man who escaped institutional confusion and became his own institution, or so the articles alleged. Of course, he was already a physical institution, carrying around a bodily weight of well over three hundred pounds; he was likewise a mental institution, since he possessed a well-advertised I.Q. that broke the intelligence barrier. His name is Herman Kahn, the human think tank, a nightmare for student radicals, a consultant to the Pentagon, and one of the few people who stood up to the furies of the age without faltering. I guess it was this last characteristic that I really admired.

In one of my truly impulsive and distraught states, I wrote the following letter, dated June 1970, to Mr. Kahn:

Dear Mr. Kahn,

I find myself an academic devoted to principles such as research and academic freedom that have been made anachronistic by the secular missionaries of a heralded "new age." This new society may be established in the name of freedom and goodness, but I don't like its odor; it has the unmistakable stench of putrifying flesh.

I've decided that a change in my position is needed—and soon. It is with this thought in mind that I have written this note. Please let me know if we may chat about that possibility at your convenience.

Sincerely,
Herb London

I also enclosed a scenario I had written in 1969 for one of my classes. It was an obviously exaggerated piece of writing that nonetheless captured my deep-seated fears about recent political movements.

Scenario:

As a result of increasing anti-war sentiment, Mr. Nixon reluctantly decides that he will unilaterally and precipitously withdraw all troops from Vietnam (before the congressional elections in 1970). Two days after this announcement, the Thieu government falls and martial law is declared in South Vietnam. Recognizing the anarchic conditions, the North Vietnamese and Viet Cong mount an offensive to completely discredit and possibly capture the entire government apparatus. Two weeks later, North Vietnamese regulars marching side by side with the Viet Cong enter Saigon and accept the terms of surrender. Two months later, reports are widely circulated throughout the world detailing communist-sanctioned slaughter of the so-called right deviationists in

South Vietnam. Ky's head is mounted on a pole and paraded through Saigon's streets.

In the United States, these reports are rejected by the left as "exaggerated reactions to unpleasant circumstances" and accepted by the right as "the consequence of capitulation." General Westmoreland appears in Madison Square Garden amid shouts of "sell out" and categorically condemns the "left wing" in the State Department, which he alleges, was responsible for his inability to conduct a victorious war. After the rally, a fight involving New Leftists and supporters of Westmoreland breaks out on Eighth Avenue. Eight people are hospitalized.

Political polarization over the war issue is quite apparent in the 1970 congressional elections. Traditional party lines are bridged as people vote for doves or hawks, terms that now have only emotional and symbolic appeal. Anti-war political muscle is manifested in a New Left party devoted to the disengagement of all American foreign troops. On the right, growing signs of a party designed to recapture American "glory" emerge, but the party does not yet have a major effect on the electorate.

However, in the two years after the congressional elections, which were heralded as a New Left victory, the right has developed into a formidable political force made up of retired generals, former Joe McCarthy supporters, and many Republicans. By 1972, this group has captured the Republican Party and nominated Reagan and Westmoreland as its candidates.

The Democratic Party, owing its success in the 1970 elections to the New Left coalition, allows this minority group to dictate policy and select its candidates. Senator McGovern and John Lindsay are nominated and Dr. Spock presents the nominating speech.

From 1969 to 1972 reports of continued slaughter in South Vietnam circulate. In addition, guerilla activity in Cambodia and Laos has forced those states to acquiesce to North Vietnamese demands. On the eve of the November 1972 presidential election Thailand falls; Tun Razak of Malaysia claims that "all of Southeast Asia is in jeopardy."

Fearful of the consequences to American security, the voters turn to Reagan and Westmoreland with an overwhelming endorse-

ment. With the executive firmly in their grasp, they introduce
martial law to deal with New Left disrupters on the streets. The
police action only incites further incidents. In twenty-two cities
across the country, the National Guard has been called in to restore
order.

In a nationally telecast statement, Reagan admits that constitu-
tional government in this country is no longer possible. A rump
congress is established, giving the President full power to effectuate policy. Twelve years later (in 1984), Reagan's son succeeds
to the presidency.

The whole enterprise was a shot in the dark; I never
expected Kahn to reply. After all, if he is the emotionless
computer that Roszak, Reich, Thompson, and other social
critics have suggested, there was simply no reason to
expect an answer. Moreover, my scenario was too easily
identifiable with Weimar Germany to make it appear
credible or to make me seem notable.

Two months later I received an invitation to the Hudson
Institute. Kahn apologized for not being able to see me
personally; he was off to the East to predict Japan's future
in the twenty-first century. But his associate and president
of the institute, Max Singer, would serve as his alter-ego.
The moment I entered the Hudson Institute at Croton-on-
Hudson, I knew I was in Kahn's Xanadu. Big, imposing,
impenetrable, the buildings reminded me of West Point
for out-of-shape cadets. The corridors were long, with
mirrors at intersections to protect you from intrepid
walkers. With Kahn's reputation, one could not help wondering whether some sophisticated monitoring system
lurked behind the mirrors. Yet despite my initial reserve,
a consequence of the imposing surroundings, I quickly
succumbed to the relaxed and friendly manner that characterized every secretary I encountered.

My first conversation was with Kahn's assistant, a thoroughly charming woman in her mid-thirties who probably graduated among the top five in her Radcliffe class. After chatting for ten minutes, she said, "You're like all of us here, a disenchanted liberal sick to death of New Left bullshit." At that moment I revised my estimate: she was class valedictorian. I immediately identified her as an unwitting product of I.C. Her penetrating analysis of my gripes and values had me wondering whether she was also Kahn's version of Arthur Clarke's computer HAL in *2001*.

Max Singer was next on the agenda. His name made him sound fiftyish, but he was a surprisingly young man. He was also the kind of man whose slender build actually made him look twenty pounds heavier than he was. When I entered his office, he was busy talking to Kahn on a long-distance call. No sooner had I sat down when he said, "London's here. What should we chat about?" Kahn replied audibly enough for me to hear: "Ask him about his article in *Orbis*. It was damn good." That thoroughly floored me. Kahn may be a genius, but I never expected him to know a thing about me, much less read one of my articles with apparent interest. Following Kahn's suggestions, Singer asked such precise questions, one would have thought that he had studied Australian immigration problems all his life. And they were uttered so quickly that I just stared at his lips, hopeful that my eyes could see what my ears had missed. I later discovered that one of Kahn's idiosyncrasies—rapid-fire speech—had been adopted by everyone on the staff. One gets the impression that every idea is allotted thirty seconds before it receives additional consideration or is rejected; so you beat the clock with verbal machine-gun power. After two hours at the Institute I was speaking like a $33\frac{1}{3}$ r.p.m. record set at 45 r.p.m. speed. Singer was also direct—very direct indeed. If he

113

was dissatisfied with one of my replies, he said, "Bullshit." Between his unintelligible questions and his discourteous shouts, I found my palms getting clammy and my impatience building. After having been interrupted three times in succession before I was allowed to finish one sentence, I shouted, "If you'll stop screaming 'bullshit' for five seconds and give me a chance to answer, you may find that I'm somewhat more knowledgeable about this subject than you think." That did it. He looked at me, turned away for an instant, and broke into a big smile. "I want you to work on a project for us," he said.

Frankness, I discovered, is something most people at the Hudson Institute value. Ten minutes after my conversation with Max, I was being introduced to another one of those charming Smith or Radcliffe women in their thirties with enough world-weariness and cleverness for ten Kathryn Ann Porter heroines. My assignment was described—very obliquely, I kept telling myself—in a manner both urgent and enthusiastic. I was asked to review Richard Blum's *Society and Drugs*, a history of drug usage, as well as to research the "best" and "most reliable" histories on the subject. Since I was not well-versed in the field of drug addiction, I approached my new job with caution—perhaps fear would be a more accurate description. I did want to impress; being at home with think tank types does have its effect.

Several minutes after my orientation, I was having lunch in a miniaturized version of an Oxfordian dining hall. Every once in a while I peered up over my food, looking for high table. Yet the friendly atmosphere and open conversation defied the formality of the room. Max could talk knowledgeably about almost anything. When I happened to mention that I had played high school and college basketball, his face brightened as if I had found a subject upon which he loved to dwell. In that austere and imposing dining room designed for benedictines of the order of the computer I discovered a soul mate. It wasn't basketball alone that was our bond; it was a concern for discipline and openness and a distaste for dogmatism.

Despite all the books I have since read that describe the Hudson Institute or Kahn, none have alluded to this feeling of openness. In an effort to confirm the stereotype of mad scientists at work, institute consultants are portrayed as impersonal automatons, unconcerned with the consequences of their actions, and oblivious to social pressures (see Paul Dickson's *The Think Tanks*). True enough, Kahn and his staff rely on scientific procedures as opposed to *I Ching*. But I for one would prefer to rely on rational arguments (rather than astrology tables) when thinking about the unthinkable. Of course, that preference is undoubtedly a result of I.C. I remain an undeviating agnostic on the matter of Edgar Cayce.

One week after this introductory session, I returned to the Institute with my report. It was all very heady stuff. For one thing, I was being held accountable for my assignment; for another, I was going to discuss my findings with a group of experts in the field; moreover, my report on drug literature was to be related to policy decisions. I can't overemphasize how dissimilar this was from an academic setting, where "accountability" is often employed by deans but unrelated to faculty action, where self-proclaimed experts on every subject lecture to colleagues as if they were eighteen-year-old sophomores, where reports on social conditions are so totally unrelated to policy concerns that one gains the impression that policy-makers are contaminated by the fallout of reality. My report was not unanimously acclaimed. Despite my effort, I could not cover in one week what some people in that seminar room had learned during twenty years of hard work. It was also very difficult to convince my listeners of the relative merits of regulated heroin distribution in Britain and Israel when doctors who had participated in both experiments were present. Nor was my discussion of the recent history of methadone maintenance programs made simpler by the presence of methadone addicts and doctors from Beth Israel hospital. It was at moments like these that I came to appreciate my freshman-class lectures.

What I also came to appreciate was a concern for practical judgments. I began to understand why Max screamed "bullshit" so often. Academic millenarianism was rarely expressed, but that was only because it was unequivocally dismissed. After years of bullshit, Max could pretty well anticipate and discourage it. It was uplifting to discuss something besides empty platitudes. Even though I had been trained in academia, after several meetings I would say "bullshit" at exactly the same moment Max exploded. When Max wanted an estimate of the effect a heroin maintenance program would have upon the illicit heroin market or the number of addicts, he expected clear, straight responses. Of course, since the possibility existed that the ideas would be translated into policy, it wasn't easy to indulge in cliché-ridden answers or simplisms derived from the experiences of a Timothy Leary.

What did come home to me as a result of this experience was the futility of so many Enlightenment suppositions about rational man. Once placed in a policy-making position, one cannot assume a standard of universal reasonableness. The drug addict can be a menace to himself and to others. In this sense, he is an archetypal primitive straining at the bit of social constraints. The characteristic "humanitarian" response to his condition is education. Educating him to reject "smack," however, is like asking me to ignore Greenberg's brownies. The hunger is not subject to reason; it recognizes only one goal: satisfaction. What often does work, at least before the addiction stage is reached, is pure, undiluted fear, fear achieved through a recognition of the consequences. It is one thing to lecture soberly about the dangers of heroin, but it is quite another, more dramatic technique, to show a photograph of an addict with pock-marked arms desperately trying to shoot up, but unable to find a functional vein. Those red lines stretching across the white background of the addict's eyes can do more to inhibit drug abuse than all the education programs in the public schools combined. I realize that fear is as out-of-fashion as ankle-length skirts and penny loafers, yet without it the liberal policy-maker can only employ dubious educational ideas or social controls envisioned in his worst nightmares. It is understandable that he opts for education as his salvation.

There are undoubtedly all kinds of drug freaks in our subculture. And I was exposed to many of them. From the needle freak who grooves on the pain of injection to the speedballer who mixes "coke" and "smack" for ups and downs—all are caught in the web of pure happiness. One addict even told me that his addiction was not merely the drug, but getting the dough to buy it.

Man, you wake up each mornin' aching for that warm feeling in your veins. But you got to go out and get one hundred bucks. You start with nothin', and you need one hundred bucks. So I begin my search. That really turns me on. I could "rip" a lock and find a cool chick or Joe Frazier. Now that keeps me goin'.

117

The realists at the Institute—and that included everyone from Kahn down—regarded such views analytically. An addict was considered something less than the symbol of pleasure that weekend "joy poppers" admired, and something more than a hopeless criminal to be relegated to a forgotten public institution. There was a desire to understand, to see the question in a larger context. It would be glib to say that ours is an addicted society. We know this to be true in a general sense, but the distinctions are what count most. The Sunday football freak is harmed less than the Baskin-Robbins addict, who is harmed less than the aspirin freak, who is harmed less than the Miltown maniac, who is harmed less than the junkie. It is also worth noting that society's attitude toward the use of drugs will determine standards of acceptability. Drug use, as well as other pleasures, is dependent on societal values. We accept alcohol as a convenient social convention conducive to conversation. We accept caffeine and nicotine as stimulants because they are consistent with our activist orientation. And we permit smoking because it satisfies an almost universal oral need. (Do you think tobacco would be legal if it were injected?) Accepted drugs are expressions of a consensual value system. My guess is that marijuana is rejected, not because it may be harmful to one's health or even to one's psychological well-being, but because the effect of the drug is inconsistent with the industrial (industrious) values of society. The more we move away from the ideas of hard work, achievement, and delayed gratification, the sooner the legalization of marijuana is likely to gain acceptance.

Kahn's Xanadu is a symbol of scientific inquiry. Perhaps that explains why it is also a symbol of impersonal technology, the betrayal of nature, and the urban plight. From what I observed, though, there is as much reason to attribute social woe to Kahn and his associates or to the Rand Corporation as there is to blame Einstein for the incineration of Hiroshima. Science is a process, a way of perceiving natural and social phenomena. It is undeniably a rational process, but one that increasingly relies upon elements of chance and possibility. It is certainly not inherently good or bad. Yet, for the new romantics, for those in the vanguard of a religious resurgence, science represents the Faustian lust for dominance. For Theodore Roszak, science is a justification for "the mad, bad ontology of our culture." It is, to use his pompous phrases, "idolatrous consciousness," "paleolithic materialism," "cultural totalitarianism," and "empiricide." It eats away at the essential beauty of nature like an insatiable parasite. It cages the mind into compartments and seals off the body from emotion. Science, for the neo-romantic, is, without question, the latest social bugaboo. To be for it is to be cut off from the energies of nature, to be hopelessly square when the invective is at its mildest, and a fascist technocrat at times when the itch for transcendence is unabated.

On a more sophisticated level, the attack upon science takes the form of a challenge of rational Newtonian assumptions that are quite susceptible to logical knock-out punches. The world, notwithstanding the Newtonians, is not a machine that can be disassembled and put together with the whole remaining equal to the sum of its parts. Many ideas of dubious value are hidden behind a cloak of "scientific law." "Penis envy," "historical determinism," and "survival of the fittest" are as easy to prove as determining whether God made Eve out of Adam's rib. Yet if the views of Heisenberg, Einstein, and, more recently, Monod have any meaning, then such meaning must lie in suspicion of pure rationality and their allowance for relativity, chance, and the non-tangible element in their calculations. Although this conclusion embodies the generally accepted direction of contemporary science, the romantics choose to ignore it. Their challenge is aimed at a science that is as anachronistic as the capitalistic system that Khrushchev vowed to bury.

Similarly, it is contended that the scientists, particularly the technocrats like Kahn, do not analyze their own assumptions. They operate, according to this view, as if all their biases are concealed behind value-free assertions. Yet pure science *is* value free: nuclear scientists warned that the results of their efforts could either lead to Hiroshima or to the desalinization of the seas, or both. And they were right. The function of knowledge is the critical element; and more often than not the decision regarding function is not left to the scientist. To play the role of moral interpreter would indeed alter the scientific profession. For then only certain investigations would be permitted; admittedly, this would eliminate many grave errors, but it would also eliminate new breakthroughs that might benefit humanity. And who makes the decisions concerning appropriate subjects for study? The Marcuseans? It is all too reminiscent of Lysenko, except that Stalinism unwittingly masquerades as neoromanticism.

The romantics, not content to stop at science, castigate those who use science for their own ends. Invariably, government is the target. On this issue, a somewhat logical point is made. Since government in a technological society is dependent upon science to pursue its policies, it can be argued that science is a tool of partisan politics. What this argument dismisses, however, is the distinction between ideas and their application, the expression of popular will that gives government legitimacy for its actions. True, government utilization of science for particular ends may offend a portion of the population, but it should also be noted that the subversion of science for environmental purposes may also be considered morally reprehensible by a portion of the population. All agencies use science for particular goals, and use implies preferences; these preferences, I would argue, will always offend someone. The key, then, in analyzing institutional decisions is the degree of openness, the willingness to listen to all sides of an argument. A closed institution and an open one may both ultimately employ science for their own purposes, but the difference between the two institutions should never be forgotten. In this obviously imperfect world, some degree of bias inevitably enters into the decision-making process. Nonetheless, it is critical that one carefully discriminate between decision makers. It can be maintained, for example, that the deflowered adolescent and the prostitute have both lost their innocence, yet the degree of loss is what ultimately counts.

Lest this account be interpreted simply as an apologia for Kahn and his associates, let me state that I began my employment with many reservations, some of which still persist in my mind. I wonder, for example, how consultants are selected? Is there a disenchanted liberal's litmus test? And if so, was I not deceived by the seeming atmosphere of openness? Yet I know that the struggles were genuine. Arguments on most matters ranged from the bizarre to the banal. For an avowed I.C. product like myself, one who is content to find the creases between the extremes, there was a good deal of space. In fact, I had more room for the expression of my ideas than was ever the case in the university.

I am bemused by Paul Dickson's account of the Hudson Institute. Surely he saw things I didn't see and perceived them differently, too. But could he be so myopic? Or is he caught in the web of counter-culture stereotypes that discourage thoughtfulness? Of course, it can just as easily be argued that I am the one who was duped. I am inclined to respect Einstein before Blake. I was predisposed to admire Kahn. And I do believe that science has done more to transcend the animal nature of man than all the divinities discovered by the gurus of Gnosticism. Yet despite it all, I am aware of my own equivocation, my usual unwillingness to embrace anything without reservations. And I was taken in.

The Hudson Institute was certainly more exciting, more attuned to actual social conditions, and more responsive to apparent needs than any academic institution I had seen. It offered me insights on a scale which I had never previously encountered. It also gave me some idea of what an academic institution could be. Kahn and his associates are not apocalyptic; they neither welcome a new age, nor are they intent on destroying this one. It is too bad that all the counter culture can see is a Dr. Strangelove bent upon total destruction. In Theodore Roszak's *The Making of a Counter Culture*, Kahn and his associates are characterized as amoral technocrats eager to accept any idea, including hippie culture and drugs, in order to maintain the *status quo*. William Irwin Thompson's *At the Edge of History* portrays Kahn as the prototypical technocrat, lacking

122

imagination and vision, yet succumbing to a positivism that allows him to foresee a future based on more of the same. The criticism is glib; in fact, despite the pretentious language, it is very reminiscent of Robert Crumb's Mr. Natural, who attacks the whole scientific establishment, or Al Capp launching into his Phoney Joannie tirade. Thompson goes so far as to compare the "vision" of Edgar Cayce with the "parochial" world-view of Kahn. That is a little like relying on tea leaves to predict the future rather than the extrapolations obtained from census data. Of course, there is the remote possibility that the tea leaves may prove correct, but until Coney Island fortune-tellers improve the accuracy of their predictions, I'll continue to place my faith in the technocrats.

My faith in science is very similar to my I.C. condition: a question of subjectivity. Science ushers in neither Utopia nor 1984; it can simultaneously relieve the burden of tiresome chores and deprive a person of the feeling of pride that is associated with a job well done. It has produced manufactured goods in vast amounts and has made them accessible to most Americans, but it has also raised the specter of "abundance for what." It implicitly suggests that "more" is better and, at the same time, demonstrates that more is worse (to borrow a phrase from Kingsley Amis). It possesses much that we desire and much that we decry. In short, it encapsulates the enigma of the age: much of what we like is also bad for us.

For I.C. products, that formed part of our heritage. Having observed cigarette smoke eating its way through Edward R. Murrow's lungs, we are somewhat less susceptible to the instant joy proclaimed by the Winchester manufacturers. But we are equally suspicious of the Luddites who promise nothing less than instant nirvana through the destruction of computers. We have observed both, and have even indulged our fantasies by willing arbitrary destruction or immediate escape to paradise. Ultimately, we make an uneasy pact with the scientists, knowing that their results can make this both the best of worlds and the worst of worlds. For those afflicted with I.C., that is a very familiar situation.

CHAPTER 9

Making Universities Conform to Nonconformity

DURING A HARANGUE with one of my students, in which I absolutely rejected the idea of offering eighteen academic credits for telepathic communication, my recently appointed assistant good-naturedly interjected, "Herb, you're the Barry Goldwater of experimental programs." I never could identify with Goldwater—the right wing always evoked fears of Westbrook Pegler in me—but that description perfectly characterized my attitude toward the programs I was asked to direct. After serving as director of experimental programs for less than a year, I could appreciate why William Shannon referred to experimental educators as the "new barbarians." From my observation, it became apparent that anything goes—as long as it is labeled "experimental." The attitude of experimenters was best captured during the following recent conversation with a director at a nearby college:

YOURS TRULY:	What activities do your students engage in when they are not taking courses?
OTHER DIRECTOR:	Crazy, man. They do everything. Of course, most of the time we have great rap sessions.
Y.T.:	But how do you know whether they get anything out of these sessions?
O.D.:	How do I know anything, man?
Y.T.:	Well, if you don't have students in conventional courses and you don't require tangible evidence of performance, how do you know when they have completed the degree?
O.D.:	Man, I just know. I just know!

As a giant lump formed in my throat, I looked at this popular, aging guru and said as politely as I could, "I think we have a different philosophical orientation. You see, I'm not quite hip; I still believe in papers, research, and assignments." Our acquaintanceship was fading rapidly. As this guy slammed the door he muttered, "That's experimental? Crazy!" If this director is at all representative, and I think he is, you can see why I readily subscribed to my designation as the Barry Goldwater of experimental education.

For someone as unattuned to the demands of this position as I was, it is curious that I got the job in the first place. My insatiable need to live several Walter Mitty lives and my I.C. sense of uneasiness in most institutional settings determined my motives. But my selection was another story.

After having been an ombudsman for a year, I paraded my battle scars like a Congressional Medal winner. I was neither universally admired nor was I vilified: limbo is a place to which I am accustomed. When a university commission was organized to investigate and reform undergraduate education, I was one of the first appointees. Since the position required one additional committee meeting a week, I greeted the news of my appointment with the same enthusiasm I reserve for filling out my annual tax statement. But there were compensations. A reformist fervor permeated our meetings. One could really get the impression that we were changing the university. It was also true that we often met at an Italian restaurant that served sensational baked clams.

After several months of meetings, we produced a document, redolent of garlic, that expressed our zeal for reform. The commission chairman, who was already an official "change agent," became the director of the first genuine experiment at the university. I was content in the knowledge that a good man had been placed in an influential position and that the cessation of committee meetings also marked the start of my much-needed diet. These results were obviously quite related to each other. However, after one month on the job, the stress of being pulled in different directions took its toll; the director rather sheepishly asked if I would assume the responsibility for educational experiments. Without any hesitation I accepted the offer. It was hardly a dramatic moment; some colleagues argued that it wasn't even an opportunity, but it certainly was different. Considering my general state of ennui at the time, that was a considerable plus.

One of the things I learned very quickly is that you shouldn't accept a new job if you have to inherit your predecessor's staff. My assistant had all the warmth of Bela Lugosi after a hard night's work. I also discovered that she had as much enthusiasm for organizing a filing system as my three-year-old daughter has for putting her toys away. As a consequence, I avoided coming to my new office for fear that I would continually ask, "Where is it?"

Fortunately, she got tired of my penetrating stares and left. Unfortunately, that meant that I had to single-handedly write a proposal for the program, design a budget, prepare a statement for the University Senate, obtain New York State accreditation, generate a publicity program, interview students, hire a faculty, gather an executive committee, and answer more questions than were asked during two decades of "Twenty Questions." Without any assistance I became an institution: I was clerk, secretary, news bureau, registrar, admissions office, bursar, program developer, and dean. For the first time I truly understood what Chairman Mao was talking about when he said, "Every leader must be a laborer." I moved furniture in the morning, typed letters in the afternoon, and made grand decisions in the evening. And it all paid off. If something went wrong, I had no one to blame but myself. To avoid creeping schizophrenia, I stopped trying to define my role. When someone asked, "What are you doing, Herb?" I replied, "Everything."

It was easier to justify what I was doing than what everyone thought I should be doing. The faculty was generally disposed to resist experimentation with varying degrees of intensity, a response that was based on dedication to some transcendent liberal arts ideal. At the first Faculty Council meeting at which I was questioned—interrogated would be a more appropriate term—a senior faculty member with prestige glistening from his whitening hair asked if I could name a great man who had obtained an external degree. It was not the sort of question I had expected; after all, the program I was defending did not offer an external degree. Moreover, I couldn't think of a great man who had obtained a conventional bachelor's degree. Yet in the back of my mind was ensconced a memory of Isaac Deutcher's biography of Lenin, in which he described Lenin's external degree program at the University of Moscow. Although Lenin's greatness is a matter of some dispute, he entered my pantheon of heroes for an instant as I blurted out, "Lenin received an external degree from the University of Moscow." Almost everyone was mildly amused, if unconvinced. Nonetheless, I had thwarted the hard questions for awhile.

On the other side of the fence were the professional experimenters, those individuals who made criticism of academia a career. At a conference on experimental education held in California (where else?), participants were asked to "stop armoring" (Reichian jargon for lowering one's defenses) by means of a sensitivity session. This approach, I was told, was the answer to the "educational doldrums." Eager to find a panacea, I willingly complied with the rules of the exercise. First, I held a portion of a puzzle in my hand while scores of people milled about in an effort to find me and a proper fit for their puzzle parts. This is presumably an important symbol for post-Freudians. Once my "cell" (since we were in Orange County, a hotbed of Birch ideas, I became a bit paranoid about the term) was organized, we were asked to select one person seated around the table and draw his (her) portrait. I proceeded to draw one fellow as diligently as I could—which was not too well. However, when the convener came by to "analyze" the results, he asked me to describe my feelings by observing my own imprecise lines. I said, "My drawing doesn't reveal very much; I draw very poorly." He replied, "That's a cop-out. That drawing reveals hate. You hate the man, but won't admit it. C'mon, admit it. You'll feel better if you do." All I could honestly admit was little aptitude for drawing. But that was obvi-

ously the wrong response. "Honesty," in this case, would
have been a dishonest "gut" response. I've come to realize
that you can often identify "sensitivity" training by its
general insensitivity. I have also come to believe that if
this is California's answer to problems of higher education, then the voters probably deserve Max Rafferty.

Confused by the neanderthals on the left and annoyed
by the rigidity of academic patricians on the right, I re-
treated into my characteristic I.C. position of invoking a
plague on both their houses. As usual, I also found myself
with very few allies. When I went to national meetings with
experimenters, they always discussed our community of
interests. But whenever I insisted that without a consistent
tuition schedule student exchange, an avowed ideal, was
impossible, I was immediately ostracized from the community. Pragmatists are not welcome among experimental
educators. Unless the former are prepared to speak the
praises of reform with the evangelical spirit of redemp-
tion, their colleagues will regard them as quislings.

The direction in which experimental education was
headed also caused me considerable dismay. Since university faculties are often rigid and high-priced, it should
come as no surprise that most experimentation avoids the
use of the regular campus offices and faculty. More often
than not, educational experiments utilize adjunct faculty
whose negligible academic qualifications are matched by
correspondingly lower salary demands. The student's
"education" continues in a community institution or
wherever else he can find it. With relatively few resources,
the student has to depend on his own ingenuity—a method
which may encourage budding Eric Hoffers or create a
generation of Uncle Hymies. It was Uncle Hymie who
always told me that experience was more important than

anything I could learn in books. Judging from my own teaching experiences in a university, the Hoffers are offering little competition to the Hymies. In fact, many universities have so extended the definition of "appropriate" educational activity that participation in student government may now earn the student four academic credits. Many universities now award credit retroactively for work experience. While the granting of credit was a needed reform for those who had educated themselves without the anguish of soporific lectures, it opened a Pandora's box of administrative headaches. How, for example, does the administrator decide which type of work is worthy of credit? Does he (she) offer credit to any one who has held that type of job or only to those who specifically apply to the program? Is it possible, or desirable, for someone to qualify for a degree without having attended any courses? These questions are not raised facetiously; surely some students should receive recognition for their informal study. But the abuses inherent in the credit-granting process remind me of a *New Yorker* cartoon in which a king announces to his subjects: "It is my wish that this be the most educated country in the world; toward that end, I hereby ordain that each and every one of my subjects be awarded a diploma."

My own professional experiences tended to reinforce my suspicions of credit being granted for life experience. One applicant requested fifty academic credits for raising four healthy sons. Another student argued that she was a superb cook, an accomplishment which she thought warranted twenty points of advanced standing. Still another contended that her philanthropic activity was "at least worth a B.A." There were no limits to the claims, unlike the narrowing limits to my patience. I do believe that the granting of credit is valid if it does nothing more than certify the years of research performed by those scholars who have labored anonymously in the dusty stacks of the New York Public Library. I have met people without high school diplomas who knew more about the Civil War than all the American history students twirling Phi Beta Kappa keys taken together. And I am also certain that one can learn more in museums, libraries, and zoos than in all the hours spent in a Philosophy I class playing "battleship." Nonetheless, not everyone wants to learn. More important, everyone's experience is not automatically translatable into academic terms.

In a society where everyone "must" have a degree, where academics are unsure of their roles, and where the student enrollment in private colleges is rapidly decreasing, reform is on the rise. Subject requirements are abandoned at the first whimper of student dissatisfaction. Grades are a legacy of the uptight fifties, a system of competitive neurosis. And professors vie for popularity by being progressive, committed, groovy, cool, with it, and even stoned, but rarely scholarly. Experimentation has become a way of keeping up with the times. The word has a magical attraction; it has been transmogrified from its ordinary usage to become a nostrum for the educational blues. I have no way of proving it, but I am firmly convinced that if Greek and Latin were offered in a so-called experimental program, students would be clamoring to enter. I've already suggested that all traditional programs be called experimental. Unfortunately, some people still take labels seriously.

On the other side of the educational barriers are the four-eyed intellectual specialists who seemingly cannot stand up without a vest. They view anything that resembles experimentation with scorn. "There is no substitute for a classical education," they insist. "People who use their hands are usually disagreeable and all but a handful of graduate students are philistines." These specialists can spend hours arguing about the exact dates of the Navigation Acts and yet experience difficulty in negotiating the passage from Manhattan to Queens. They can write book-length critiques of Norman Mailer, but wouldn't be found dead drinking a draft of beer with him at the Lion's Head. It is also this group that invariably views any modification in standards as the thin edge of the wedge of philistinism. For them, the sixties was a nightmare, a bad dream they hope to avoid in the seventies through additional committee meetings. Of course, their suspicions are well-founded, but their actions are hopelessly naive. Even the most productive hours of nit-picking research will not transport them out of the twentieth century. Their adamant posturing against reform is so predictable that the experimenters have little to react against except anachronistic ideas. And that is the rub. The critics of reform have a role to play *as* critics. They can mitigate the unabashed enthusiasm for the novel yet, at the same time, offer some constructive suggestions instead of merely rejecting reform.

Having labored in the field of educational experimentation for a short but significant period of time, I thought I would share my findings with others. I was not egotistical enough to believe that what I wrote would make a difference, yet an irrepressible optimism forced me to try. After having visited several college programs that were advertised as being experimental, I wrote an article for *The Saturday Review*, the most popular educational journal in the country. To my surprise, it was published. And that's when things began to happen. Although the article was, in my view, well-balanced, several experimenters argued that I had broken the faith. I was branded as a turncoat who had violated "the trust and openness" of experimental programs in a way that "demonstrated [my] irresponsibility." One friend who had read some of the critical letters I received sympathetically noted, "Now I know what Melvin Laird wrote to Daniel Ellsberg after the publication of the Pentagon Papers." I was criticized for using egregious examples (all of them were true, and by no means exaggerated); I was vilified for extracting information under false pretenses (of course, I had no intention of writing an article when I visited the institutions in question); and I was condemned for being an educational reformer who condemned educational reformers. In one month's time I had become *persona non grata* at national meetings of experimental educators, and when I heard two reformers chatting about "the bastard," I knew precisely who they had in mind.

This wasn't the only problem, though. The patricians had read my article as selectively as had the reformers. All they could see was "a ludicrous matter" being taken seriously by a "semi-literate educationist." As far as they were concerned, the article wasn't a matter worth considering, except for those who have little else to do with their time but hatch schemes to destroy the university. They did embrace several of my negative criticisms as confirmation of their prejudices, but they rejected my conclusions as a product of misguided zealousness.

Still, I have found that the role of experimental educator suits me. As usual, most people don't understand my motives, nor I theirs. We work side by side, but at crosspurposes. Like so much that had preceded the furor over the article, I suspect that this, too, is a function of I.C.

I always liked going to school and I always liked to learn. Sure, I took basketball more seriously than physics, but I still recall that mass equals weight times velocity and that if one is driving a car there's a good reason to recall that equation. I also knew that some guys were dumb—the word has fallen into disuse—and some were smart. If I wanted to learn something or to borrow someone's homework, it wasn't from the local Denny Dimwit. I also knew that some experiences belonged in a school and some indubitably didn't. I remember pitching pennies in the school yard and taking bets on whether or not three baseball players would get a total of six hits, but I would have been eligible for Happy Home if I considered these experiences worthy of academic credit. While in college, I wrote poetry, painted, and traveled, but I wouldn't have had the nerve to suggest that these activities represented learning experiences. As is the case with most college students, my poetry resembled badly written Gibran with a dash of existential *Angst*; my painting echoed late Kandinsky without the early stages, and my travels confirmed George Bernard Shaw's axiom, "You can take an ass around the world, but it won't become a horse." In short, I was a fairly typical student.

What makes me unusual—if I may be self-indulgent— is my continued admiration for standards that are generally rejected by my peers. Very few students are willing to do hard academic work. The best evidence of this is that, in all the research papers I've read, not one student has been able to demonstrate an appreciation of research techniques. Grand theories, paradigms, models, and proposals are proffered as if generalizations are synonymous with conclusions. But where is the student who still engages in the unglamorous job of serious research? He is probably

writing books like this one, without even a modest gesture
to the anonymous academics who make popular works
possible.

Experimental education may be right for the person who
can study without much guidance. But it is unfair to the
average student to propagate the myth that any moderately
resourceful person can educate himself. In my experimental programs there are people who perform well; but they
are invariably individuals who have a sense of discipline,
a capacity to work independently, and a maturity that
enables them to continue after the first disappointment.
Paul Goodman's notion that anyone can learn how to read
ignores the extraordinarily high illiteracy rates that obtained before compulsory education was instituted. Likewise, the popular wisdom which suggests that education is
a charade which enslaves the individual more than it liber-
ates him is refuted by every academic who, two genera-
tions ago, would have left his *shtetl* at a great risk to life
and limb. There is a distinction between *E*nslavement and
*e*nslavement, and all the Marcusean logic cannot eradicate
the difference.

Experimental education emerged in the sixties as a
response to the so-called desensitizing trap of college,
job, success, family, wealth, and frustration. That was the
inexorable ontogeny of middle-class America and the cancer of its children. As the identity crisis became more
fashionable, the multiversity grew less acceptable. Education became more than an exposure to the great books;
it was a way of "finding oneself." If one expression characterized the period, that was it. In the seventies, it has
become chic to say, "I'm putting it together," but in the
sixties mothers in Miami Beach hotels would say, "My

son Herbie is finding himself." It makes you wonder where his "self" was all these years.

Most of the time, the finding of oneself occurred at an educational institution and, with increasing frequency, in an experimental program. It wasn't that experimentation made the search any easier; it was just that experimental programs allowed you to do things besides study. It used to be that you took a trip and considered it a vacation, an interlude from study; now it is interpreted as the study itself. If there is anything that makes the older generation angry, it is being told that play is study and vice versa. While eating lunch in Dubrow's Cafeteria on Seventh Avenue, a man in his fifties turned to his friend and said, "I'm supporting my son to be a playboy; he calls it experimental education. Experimental my ass."

Few things change attitudes more quickly than a recession. With belt-tightening more prevalent today than a decade ago, the trends described by most social commentators may be little more than aberrational shifts. One now has to take three courses on how to pass a law school entrance exam; the debris from medical school applications could be used for a ticker tape parade up Broadway more impressive than the one held to celebrate MacArthur's return from Korea. Maybe that is the actual trend. Yet experimentalism gains in popularity even as medical school applications soar. Perhaps five years from now there will be nothing but experimental programs and medical schools—and, after ten years have passed, we may have experimental programs *in* medical schools. At that point we may be saying, "Heaven help the patient with a doctor who is trying to find himself."

Experimental education, like almost anything else, is as

good or as bad as the experimenters. There is nothing inherently wrong with experimentation—with the exception of unsubstantiated claims made in its behalf. Perhaps it is worth recalling the obvious: every accepted practice was once an experiment. Yet for an I.C. type like myself, there is something objectionable about all the furor. I was and still am a confirmed skeptic on this matter. Before I take a hard line one way or the other, I'll need many more answers.

CHAPTER 10

A Cross-Eyed Look at the Last Two Decades

I'M STILL LOOKING for the place where I belong. I guess I'll always be looking. This is not my *On the Road*; Kerouac, after all, was trying too hard to be different, but in the end he gravitated to all the truly "different" Americans in Hollywood. My odyssey is more typical, I think; it is characterized by congested streets, ghetto schools, teen-age dreams, and the national drama of the last ten years.

I consider the election held in 1960 as my "awakening." Kennedy was my Lancelot; he was a welcome contrast to the stasis of the Eisenhower years. I began the decade as a social democrat devoted to the ideas of the Enlightenment. Despite a disinclination to argue, I could defend the ideals of Jefferson, Eugene Debs, and Stevenson with all the fervor of a fire-and-brimstone sermonist. My political cosmology was simple: the Socialists and those with related philosophies were good, Conservatives and Republicans were bad. There were, of course, some aberrations. Willkie wasn't all bad, but he certainly wasn't a Roosevelt either. From my point of view, voting for a Republican was like rooting for the New York Yankees. Kids from Brooklyn just didn't do things like that, not if they wanted to remain intact.

When Kennedy was killed, my world was shattered. I had always suspected that man is not perfectible, but the assassin's irrationality drove that lesson home. Still, I was open to any ideology as long as the rhetoric suggested good intentions. I viewed SDS as an extension of the League for Industrial Democracy, a kind of nursery school for youthful Marxist dilettantes. Little did I suspect that it would spawn bomb factories, riots, and four-letter epithets that leave a soapy taste in my mouth whenever I use them. I identified with the "freedom rides" in Mississippi, freedom marches, and demonstrations, but I could not for the life of me endorse "Burn, baby, burn" or "Off whitey." I was hopelessly liberal; I wanted the millennium without the bloodshed. There was a time at the start of the sixties when I could proudly describe myself as a radical. By the mid-sixties I sheepishly answered to the description "moderate." Now, however, with the times so overheated, a moderate is a fence-sitter, a passionless Caspar Milquetoast unable to make political choices. That certainly isn't me. So with all the bravado of the age, I have labeled myself a "militant centrist." To my surprise, it works. When I say "militant," most people don't even listen to the rest of the label; they just nod affirmatively. I am certainly no different from the moderate I was several years ago, but my label makes it seem so.

My political ideology, to the extent that I have one, was nurtured in an age when opposing views were respected. The presumed goal of debate was to learn and possibly even go through the painful process of changing an opinion. Since most of my Marxist cronies knew woefully little about economics—who read *Das Kapital* anyway?—a bull session was very much like hashing over a primer on the theory of supply and demand. To be political in those days was to be relatively open. Of course, I preferred arguments that confirmed my suppositions and, when placed on the defensive, I was not above personal vilification. I still react the same way. But what I don't understand is the present unwillingness to engage an adversary. To win is to shout him (her) down. Radicals consider debate an empty exchange of ideas that inhibits action. "Better to be wrong and committed than to be right and uncommitted," is the underlying argument of much contemporary political thought. Perhaps the decade required more action than reflection, but for an I.C. type all the fancy rhetoric and appeal to the good cause could not justify mindless acts of destruction. On several occasions I heard rioters explain that their destructive acts were symbolic gestures against property and caused no harm to people. However, if I had to choose between preserving a manuscript that took two years of hard labor to compose or losing a little finger, I'm not sure which way I'd turn. The fact is, I just don't use my pinky that much.

I.C. also implies an intuitive respect for proprieties. A society like ours, with all its imperfections, is based upon a social compact that requires observance of some mutually shared values. Sure, values are changing, and just as surely the social compact seems less stable today than it did two decades ago, but my concern for proprieties is stamped on the cerebrum as a sign of my generational viewpoint. And all the rallies and marches and "touchy-feely" sessions are not likely to change that. My students, and even many contemporaries, call me uptight, a strange bird who won't fly free with the rest of the peregrines. They are right, but I cannot fly unless I know my destination.

For those at the barricades the sixties represented a struggle for liberation. In the name of liberation every convention was discarded, as easily as old newspapers. And who could resist the appeal? "Liberate the university from professorial tyrants"; "Liberate women from their enslavement by men"; "Liberate the people from an unresponsive government"—the shouts resonated through the corridors of the nation. Yet all the while the goal remained unclear. Liberation, for those who proclaimed its virtues, is a delusion, a function of perceptual woe. It is the thing to say, a panacea for disenchanted students, mothers, and citizens. Yet it is, as every philosopher from Plato to Erich Fromm knows, so elusive.

Perhaps the following story, which has been repeatedly enacted, best demonstrates the point I am trying to make. A young secretary with relatively few skills and no high school diploma was employed by my urban university as a departmental secretary. Since she worked for "permissive" academics, her workday usually began at 10 A.M. and ended prematurely at 4 P.M. There was also a two-hour midday interlude for lunch that even the Romans would have considered excessive. Despite many typing errors and an uncalled-for rudeness when answering telephone calls, she was never reprimanded. In fact, she felt sufficiently relaxed to call every professor by his or her first name. One day, quite unexpectedly, she announced her decision to leave. When I asked her the reason, she said that it had nothing to do with her salary, which was appallingly low, but with "the repression in the office." She claimed that "the job didn't fit into my schedule; I couldn't feel free and hold this position." Unwilling to assume the role of a Simon Legree, I wished her well as she went on her way. Several months later, I ran into her. "What are you doing?" I asked. "Oh, I joined a commune in Brooklyn. For the first time in my life I feel really liberated." Intrigued by her reply, I asked about her work and her new role. "Since everyone in the house but me is an artist, I keep house. I get up with the kids (five, to be exact) at 6 A.M., prepare breakfast, do the dishes, shop, make lunch, take the kids to the playground, prepare dinner, do the dishes, play with the kids, put them to bed, smoke a joint, and conk out. I'm usually so tired, I can't wait to sleep. But it's great, really great. If only everyone could be this free."

If this actual episode proves anything, it is the fact that objective conditions are irrelevant whenever feeling, not logic, are in control. The search for meaning has led the products of Con III to the Orwellian world of doublethink. Liberation is enslavement; repression is permissiveness. If Nixon is guilty of dissimulation—and who can deny it?— so are those individuals who, in their efforts to feel better, prefer to see only shadows on cave walls. The search for meaning in the seventies represents an effort to discover an orthodoxy. It can be the catechism of Marcuse, the Jesus Freaks, Charles Manson, or Zen. As long as the idea is presented with conviction, it is believable.

To the products of I.C., this phenomenon is equivalent to viewing *Brave New World* in cinemascope. Orthodoxies are to be shunned. Even our brand of Marxism rejected orthodoxy. We emerged from the postwar era knowing full well that Hitler was wrong—as was Stalin—but it was hard to know what was right. We believe in a process called the American political system, yet we also know that it tolerates many inequities and perpetuates various evils. (Watergate is hardly the first and certainly not the last.) But we continue to believe in the system because the recent past has made the alternatives so unpalatable. I.C. rejects the conservative axiom that whatever is, is right, but it is equally critical of the radical claim that whatever is, is wrong. For us, both are right and wrong. Although I have come to the conclusion that history progresses at a glacial pace, I am emotionally unwilling to live complacently with social problems. I am a radical conservative torn by the competing tendencies of logic and justice.

I can think of one apparent and appropriate analogue for my situation. Conservatism is like fishing in a lake which is free of turbulence. The sounds and movements are predictable as one glides along, pulled forward by a seemingly inexorable force. One feels rooted in time and space, an object in harmony with its natural surroundings. Radical thought, on the other hand, is like fishing in a rushing brook whose sharp rocks make one's footing a precarious affair. The risks are great, but so is the excitement. One feels out of tune with nature, a force challenging the natural flow of things. But the euphoria of the moment makes everything else seem unimportant.

I.C. captures something of both, but without the assurance of the conservative or the complete exhilaration of the radical. The state of I.C. is selective. Although discrimination is of prime concern to products of I.C., this fact should not suggest a completely positive picture. I.C. types are haughty; some are even consumed by an inner sense of superiority. Of course, it's easy to be this way; superiority is not just a hallmark of I.C. More often than not, I.C. is characterized by reflection, not action. If I.C. types are experiencing a revolution, it is a "revolution of thought," to borrow a phrase from Jacques Ellul. We want to understand the so-called dramatic changes in our society, but we rarely feel ourselves to be a part of them and often wonder just how dramatic they really are. Most of us are skeptics; and a few, like myself, are inveterate cynics. Perhaps that's what it takes to maintain a semblance of psychological equilibrium at a time when television hails the introduction of any new product or discovery as the cure, for everything from unhappiness to boredom. But it makes us fit targets for the charge: "If you know so much, why aren't you making this a better world?" I.C. products are open to such accusations. But we also feel confident that, regardless of one's actions and degree of dedication, no one person or group of persons is likely to make this a much better world. You can see why I am an inveterate cynic.

That very cynicism serves as the social compass for I.C. types. We observe the ebb and flow of history rather passively because we suspect that there is a balancing principle which makes the excesses less excessive and the crises less critical. As discontented groups threaten to abandon the nation, blow it up, or purge it of the Commies, we admittedly suffer some, yet we manage to cope. The events of the sixties were no less exasperating to us than they were to the marchers and the followers of George Wallace, yet we instinctively recognized a dialectic that signaled a return to stability after a period of turbulence. I guess it's very much like an old baseball axiom: "If you wait long enough, the good hitters will get their hits." History follows its own peculiar highway—a conclusion, I might add, embraced by both Marxists and Burkeans—one which has fewer detours than Abbie Hoffman would have us believe. And this is so because of the contradictions inherent in change. A war on poverty designed to eliminate extreme class differences may achieve its goal; but if it does, the relative differences in class income will be exaggerated. Almost every Park Avenue resident recognizes the invidious distinction of having a chauffeur or a custom-made Rolls Royce. This does not mean that effort to achieve an egalitarian society is futile; it merely suggests that the issue is not always solved by direct human action. If the sixties proved anything, it proved that political solutions rarely resolve fundamental social problems. When they succeed, a nasty situation is temporarily controlled; when they fail, the problems spill over. But the incongruities always remain, and I.C. makes us aware of them. As a nation we are crude and refined; idealistic and money-grubbing; arrogant and self-critical. Our apologies are abject and courageous; our declarations are part braggadocio and part insecurity. Our pacifism increases as we become more violent. We have fewer answers, yet more and more people assume authoritative airs. There are well-meaning incompetents and mean-spirited experts. Things are both better and worse. If you call for the time in New York you dial NERVOUS; in San Francisco the code name is POPCORN. At this moment, I.C. is a ball of incongruities that incorporates these extremes. During most of the sixties these contradictions were hidden by the erratic character of the popular culture; but with the gradual slowing down of the movement, I.C. has once again become visible.

An issue like feminism has all the earmarks of incongruity that typify I.C. To the extent that the movement challenges unequal pay, lack of recognition for a mother's role, and limited career options, it is endorsed as a reasonable social plan. But when, in its extreme form, it discloses a pathological hatred of men, an unwillingness to recognize biological differences, and labels mothers as pigs, feminism becomes an oddity, a social movement having as much clout as the vegetarian lobby.

Similarly, I.C. types have a visceral dislike for the compensatory gestures that are meant to rectify historical evils, yet inflict contemporary social evils. Racism, notwithstanding all the arguments of William Kunstler and Eldridge Cleaver, is not eliminated by excusing the wrongs of Yahoos or modifying the rules for blacks. And most blacks—even those who want a fast piece of the action—know that. Soon after I had resigned as university ombudsman, a young black student sought me out in order to file a general indictment against the college. Despite the fact that I was no longer in a position to effectuate change, I agreed to listen.

For four years I've attended this college. I've compiled a B+ average and have won a scholarship each year; yet in all the time I've been here I have not been asked to write one paper, read one book, or do any research. My work, if you can call it that, has consisted of talking about my ghetto experiences in every class I've taken. If I can get a B.A. for talking about the ghetto, then my grandmother, who has lived there for sixty years and knows a hell of a lot more about it than I do, should be given an honorary Ph.D.

I.C. products might wonder why this student stuck it out for four years, but one still ought to commend his honesty and his ability to perceive the educational hoax. Just because the rules have changed doesn't mean that blacks are unaware of the alteration. By placing a group in the position of not being able to achieve a modicum of success through hard and diligent work, new shackles are

147

forged to replace the old. I think it was Tolstoy who said that "the difference between right-wing and left-wing oppression is like the difference between dog shit and cat shit." That may not be a literal translation, but I'm sure the point is clear enough.

As I hope I have illustrated, I.C. is not strictly a function of age, although those between the ages of twenty-seven and thirty-seven are most likely to recognize this condition in themselves. Nor is I.C. related to shared experience. Certainly, the events which I have reported here are idiosyncratic, a result of my own background; they could not be duplicated, either individually or in combination, by anyone else. I.C. is also not directly related to geography, although it is easier for New Yorkers (or residents of any large city) to identify with its spirit. What counts, what gives I.C. its special character, is the social context in which events of the last two decades have taken place: sirens in the night, accusatory fingers on the television screen, men with heavy beards, candlelight vigils, singing "We Shall Overcome," rooting for Willie Mays, napalm flames, flowered Volkswagen buses, and eyes that stare intensely.

These memories, however, are not what sets I.C. apart; they can be recalled by any adult who has lived through the sixties. It is the way in which the events were perceived. The Who breaking their guitars on the Fillmore stage in 1970 was not the final word in existential destruction; this group was merely an extension of Little Richard's concerts at the Brooklyn Paramount. Goldwater is not the fiend of reaction; whatever values he may have represented in 1964 were a resurrection of the spirit of Robert Taft. Bob Dylan may be the poet laureate of this age, but what would he have been without Leadbelly and

148

Woody Guthrie? Would bell bottoms have been possible without the naval tradition? Is there a Richard Brautigan without a Lawrence Ferlingetti? A James Cozzens without an Ayn Rand? Those individuals who retain a sense of the past—and there aren't that many of us left—recognize an active bond uniting us with history that makes all the well-advertised differences between the Age of Aquarius and the past no different from what we had known before.

The problem with the sixties generation, if I may describe it as a problem, is its lack of a historical perspective. History for Jerry Rubin began with the Tonkin Bay Resolution. As a result, every event is judged unique, every work of art is unparalleled. It is existentialism without existentialism's implicit responsibility for human behavior. A sense of history also explains why I.C. progeny don't get exhilarated over Andy Warhol; why water pistols in the senate chamber seem bizarre at best; and why droopy mustaches remind us as much of Trotsky or Zapata as John Lennon. Because we view history as a seamless web of events, we are more philosophical, and consequently less romantic. Our passion is somehow less fiery and our heroes are less swashbuckling.

It is impossible to predict how those who share the spirit of I.C. will respond to any specific issue. My guess is that I.C. types in 1972 were equally divided among McGovern and Nixon supporters on the one hand, and non-voters on the other. We might enjoy a short story in *Playboy*, agree with a Norman Podhoretz editorial, or think Wittgenstein provocative. But we are, above all, unpredictable. We are probably not Godard freaks, but we certainly don't boycott foreign films. We travel when the opportunity arises, but we usually don't view France as the promised land. Exaggerated bell bottoms and garishly patterned

149

shirts might turn us off, but flared trousers and pointed collars are tastefully stylish and acceptable. We don't eat lunch at Lutèce, yet we find Horn and Hardart less acceptable now that it has been taken over by the junkies. In short, we are not trying to be what Madison Avenue, a C.B.S. documentary, or the East Side crowd demands that we be.

There is no wholeness to I.C., no chain of commitments in which one broken link automatically destroys continuity. We share the values that come from selecting, but our sharing does not make any standard de rigueur. Middle America may demand conformity—radical chic clearly does—but I.C., both by definition and in spirit, implies diversity. If that is a cop-out, a sign of my lack of commitment, I accept my guilt. But as I see it, it is better to be culpable than phony. I won't conform because of any pressure to conform. That is my position—and it is unalterable.

Like all I.C. products, my formative years occurred during the fifties and sixties. The decades were as different in character as James Garner's roles in *Cash McCall* and *The Americanization of Emily*. In ten years an obvious super-hero became a cowardly anti-hero. Of course, the decades were not as different as the mass media has implied. But the differences that did exist were so closely juxtaposed that they took on an exaggerated quality. If the sixties had been the eighties, all the tumult would have been scaled down. It was this seeming explosion of values that resulted in I.C.; eclecticism is a natural consequence of apparent polarities. In terms of style, I.C. borrowed from both periods; it is part *Captain Video* and part *Underdog*.

If the advance notices of the seventies are accurate, I suspect that an age of neo-conservatism is upon us. And that presages an I.C. generation in the eighties which will undoubtedly seek a synthesis between Frank Zappa and Mr. Make No Waves of the seventies. This book may, in a decade, be rewritten by some crew cut who has self-consciously let his sideburns grow, or by a Columbia revolutionary employed by I.B.M. The forms may change, just as all styles change, but the resulting intergenerational confusion will probably still be the same.

I'm sure that everyone who eats hamburgers at MacDonald's *and* Daly's Dandelion, as I do, doesn't share my uneasiness about how stylistically different they are. That may be unique. But I do know that there are others like myself who feel uncomfortable in settings where only the beautiful and chic set can be seen, or in places where only blue-collar workers who preface every remark with "fuckin' " can be heard. I simply cannot embrace either and still remain true to myself. Yet my inability to identify with a particular group leaves me estranged, an estrangement exacerbated by the mass media, which has adopted the convenient habit of stereotyping extremist groups. To some extent, I am guilty of this same charge. I.C. is a stereotype, but it is also a very personal reaction to the last two decades; it is a moderate's cry for recognition while presumed experts are busily characterizing recent history solely in terms of radical actions. What I want to shout, in a voice only marginally louder than my normal speaking tone, is: "Hey, how can you talk about this nation and leave me out?" That's what I.C. represents, and I think there may be others like myself who want to ask the same question.

Glossary

THIS BOOK was obviously written by a New Yorker for New Yorkers. Its flavor and tone reflect the distinctive qualities of this city. To maximize the pleasures (and discomforts) to be derived from the reading of this book, a glossary has been included.

Caution should be exercised in its use, however. For example, readers in Cleveland, Ohio, unlike New Yorkers, can hardly be expected to know that "three sewers" constitutes a home run in stickball; and "color war" would probably be construed as a reference to race riots by the vast majority of Americans. What follows, then, should give the reader an accurate, but strictly personal, definition of key terms.

Alan Freed was Mr. WINS himself, host of the first and foremost rock station in all New York. He made rock music for me. He was irreverent, unpredictable, and the only part-black, part-Jewish disc jockey I ever heard of. He not only gave rock a life in New York, he invented payola.

Azuma is a Japanese head shop that sells every conceivable *chatchka* for teen-agers and unreconstructed teen-agers (i.e., those individuals who are past the normal age limit yet still play at being young) who want the vicarious joys of sex and drugs. For the low, low price of ten dollars one can buy a calendar that not only gives you the date, but graphically illustrates the 101 positions of sexual intercourse.

Bar Mitzvah Speech. A ritual usually undertaken by thirteen-year-old Jewish boys. It nets you a lot of gifts and money, and it grants something to your parents called *nachas*. Most of the time the rite is a magical performance that surprises the speechmaker, who, after six months of listening to a record three hours a day, memorizes the speech with only three errors. At age thirty-four he can still deliver the same speech with only two errors, a fact that still brings a smile to the lips of his proud parents.

Baseball Record Book. The bible for Brooklyn males between the ages of ten and twelve. Like rabbinical scholars, they discuss the nuances of every statistic for hours. For example, a conclave of baseball rabbis was recently held on Avenue Y in Brooklyn to discuss the implications of Hank Aaron's quest for Babe Ruth's home run record. There was no consensus, as one might expect, but it gave everyone a chance to guess who held the record before the Babe, as well as other assorted facts.

These record-keepers are not usually good students, and

154

in many cases they aren't even good athletes. But their relentless quest for trivial facts makes them appear exceptional to everyone except their parents. Dad just can't understand how his kid can get a "D" in history and yet remember that the National League was officially organized in 1876.

Baskin-Robbins. Some New Yorkers now maintain that Baskin-Robbins has the best ice cream in the city. That's probably because they haven't eaten Häagen Dazs. Nonetheless, Baskin-Robbins is not a distant second and its Rocky Road is unparalleled.

Battleship is a game played by making lots of dots on a blank piece of paper, assigning numbers to those dots, and then attempting to conceal a ship on the board while your opponent sends out depth charges in the form of numbers. It's not as complicated as it sounds; and in fact, it is the best therapy for students who find classroom lectures rather boring.

Bloomingdale's is "home" for the East Side set. It is the only place in New York where single, unattached women feel truly comfortable. Advertising itself as a department store, it is really a womb with free make-up treatments. Every beautiful New Yorker can be found there. Even the sales clerks look as if they had stepped out of the pages of *Vogue*. If Bloomingdale's is selling it—even if it happens to be fur-lined roller skates—you can be sure that fur-lined roller skates are in this year.

Board of Education Guidelines are the result of what educators can do after playing with a Ouija board for fifty years.

155

Boys' High School, at one time, attracted the best minds in the city; now it attracts the best basketball players. Boys' name is synonymous with a low college entry rate and many "city championships."

Brighton Beach is sometimes referred to as the Miami of the North—by those who take hallucinogens. Brighton is where old people sit on boardwalk benches, staring at the ocean and dreaming of their youth. Every day they take the same slow stroll from Ocean Parkway to the Democratic Club on Fourth Street. It is a haven for the followers of Abe Beame—and for muggers, who can easily overtake the aged on their predictable strolls.

You can be sure you're in Brighton when any conversation of more than five minutes' duration turns to "my son the millionaire, why doesn't he visit me?" There are almost as many millionaires discussed in Brighton Beach as there are Palestinians who claim that they were not compensated after the 1948 Mideast conflict.

Bronx High School of Science undoubtedly attracts the brightest kids in the city—and the worst basketball players.

Brooklyn Dodger Fans are a fanatical breed of baseball fans who, for example, waited hours on Bedford Avenue to catch a Duke Snider home run ball. With the departure of the Dodgers from Brooklyn, the fans scattered. Some became followers of the Knicks and the Mets, but most simply wander around Brooklyn in search of someone with whom to share memories of a glorious past— Jackie dancing off first, Campy squatting behind the plate, Gil with those beautiful hands, and Pee Wee's shuffle step

156

in front of a ground ball. For the Dodger fan, life has never been the same since 1958. They live for nostalgia—and hope that maybe one day they will be able to wrap their hands around Walter O'Malley's neck.

The Brooklyn Paramount was the center for fifties rock freaks. It was a place for Murray the K, Little Richard, Dion and the Belmonts, The Cleftones, Bo Diddley, dancing in the aisles, and tearing up your seat. It was the only theater in New York where you could see *Blackboard Jungle* on the screen and dance to "Rock Around the Clock" in the aisles. Although it is now the home of Long Island University's Brooklyn branch, you can, if you press your ear against the wall and listen carefully, still hear Little Richard singing "Long Tall Sally."

Bubble Gum are rock lyrics that are even too sophisticated for five-year-olds raised on Grimms' *Fairy Tales*. Invariably, "bubble gum" lyrics are interlarded with such profound expressions as "you baby you, shu be do."

C, if you're an I.C. product, always meant a satisfactory, if not a very good, academic performance. One didn't exactly do a Snoopy dance over a C, but neither would one throw oneself over the Palisades. However, in the age of equality, where undifferentiated grades often characterize academic evaluations, the only grades one sees with regularity are A's and B's. It is no wonder, then, that a C is tantamount to an F. It is also no wonder that, in 1970, seventy-five percent of the student population at the university where I was employed were on the Dean's list. Cleverly, the Dean changed the title of this dubious honor to the "List." He could have simply called it a student roster.

Casa Mama's refers to any pizza parlor which serves slices so piping hot that you can't be sure whether it's cheese that is dripping down your fingers or the remains of the roof of your mouth. Invariably, it was the place to take a date after a movie or to celebrate a basketball victory. It was also the place where you could count on meeting the former boyfriend of the girl you were presently dating.

Change Agent has no relation to the dispenser of change in New York City's subway system. Rather, he is the person designated by static bureaucratic institutions to assume responsibility for the condition of stasis.

Chip Hilton was a literary character created by Clair Bee, former basketball coach at Long Island University, and his ghost writer. Hilton did everything I ever dreamed of doing on an athletic field—and then some. He was the only fictional character who won 120 letters. Of course, it took him sixteen years to get out of college.

Chuck Berry was the black Presley. Every record he made was pure gold. His "car songs" (e.g., "Maybelline") made "cruising" a national sport. Even the Beatles admitted the debt they owed him for the unique guitar harmonies in his records. His lyrics weren't avant-garde—he was hardly what one would describe as revolutionary, despite his arrest record—but there was a wildness in his songs that was usually expressed by "putting the top down" and "peeling out."

Chutzpah. People who have chutzpah are definitely at an advantage; those who have to deal with these individuals usually develop a case of high blood pressure. Simply stated, chutzpah is borrowing a friend's car and then complaining that it doesn't have a full tank of gas.

The City Championship. Any kid in the city of New York recognizes that the City Championship is the most coveted award he could ever receive, for New York is where the best players play. The annual game serves as a preview of future college All-Americans and professional stars—if the players don't become drug addicts first.

The Coasters. For six years, from 1954 to 1960, that is, when I was in high school and college, every Coaster record seemed to be a hit. I can still remember the dates of the Coasters' big hits during that era. And even though it may seem unlikely, songs like "Charlie Brown" were the inspiration for Bob Dylan's "Subterranean Homesick Blues."

Color War. By splitting the entire summer camp population in half and imposing a theme, e.g., North vs. South, a competition bordering on bloodlust could be generated among all campers over four years of age. For two solid weeks these sides competed in everything from marching formations and athletic contests to singing songs and making beds. The amazing thing about this competition was that every year, without fail, some schlump who had been written off as a hopeless bungler did something miraculous to win a game and add one-half point to his team's score. His mother was usually grateful; his grandmother gave the counselor a twenty dollar tip, and the kid returned to camp the following summer.

Daly's Dandelion is an East Side restaurant for guys wearing well-tailored leather pants and hairdos styled at Alfieri's. The women are trim, wear embroidered jeans, and talk without moving their lips—when they do talk, which is rare. As you might have guessed, the drinks are overpriced, the hamburgers oversized, the music played most frequently is by the Grand Funk Railroad, and the bodies are pushed close together by the crowd at the bar in what often resembles the orgy planned for the following evening.

Darien Dudes are distinguished-looking, white-haired gentlemen who drink martinis with a twist, are obsessed with something called a handicap, can be found riding the New York-New Haven line at 10:15 A.M., and prefer their secretaries to their wives.

David Cassidy is last year's heartthrob for teen-age girls too young to have been weened on "I Want to Hold Your Hand." (Is that possible?) This young man, like so many of his predecessors, has managed to mold a television persona, a pretty-boy appearance, and almost no talent into something called a career, more accurately described as "the manufactured annual crush image."

Denny Dimwit, a comic strip character, was the town buffoon. His pointed hat was probably the source of the expression "pinhead"—commonly used to describe the dumbest people one knew. During the 1940's and 1950's, this was one comic strip you didn't overlook in the pages of the *New York Sunday News*.

De Witt Clinton High School is the Bronx's answer to Boys' High. In recent years it has even supplanted Boys' as the number one basketball factory in New York City.

Dubrows. Although there are several Dubrows in the city, I always associate the name with the Seventh Avenue restaurant located in the garment center, where more than half of the patrons speak Yiddish and where a majority of the conversations are about the *"Kinder."* During the ephemeral flower people age, one could see long-haired youths sitting uneasily with their parents, with one ear listening to dad's advice about hair and drugs and the other picking up mom's suppressed sobs. Before junior returned to his Delancey Street pad, the one that his old man had left a generation earlier, he took the ten-dollar bill that was surreptitiously placed in his hand.

Elton John, a rock singer with a name that sounds reversed, is this year's heartthrob for rock aficionados. His "Daniel" does combine reasonable lyrics and melody, but that fact alone doesn't explain his popularity. As with most rock singers, he exudes the requisite sexual attraction for teen-age girls.

Eric Bentley, a drama instructor, formerly of Columbia University, without really trying became something of a hero among student activists during the late sixties.

In one of the most vindictive reviews I have ever read, Bentley excoriated Norman Podhoretz for trying to "make it" with the New York literati. After all, he argued by implication, who but a reactionary would want to make it in this fascist-ridden, dictatorial, capitalist-controlled, sexually frustrated society. Bentley is now a well-paid professor reaping the psychic and financial rewards provided by his elevated station.

Fabian, a pretty boy from Philadelphia, had little singing talent, but an excellent manager. After several abortive recording efforts, he got a Hollywood contract. He is now making films that are generally panned by the critics but admired by most teen-age girls.

Fillmore East, advertised as a rock concert hall, was actually the world's largest opium den. It also had the most creative bookings of any rock concert hall in the world. Regardless of what one might think of these rock events, The Who's rendition of *Tommy* and *Jesus Christ Superstar* were first presented on the Fillmore stage.

Forty-Second Street Storefronts are the places where *Everything you always wanted to know about sex but were afraid to ask* can be learned without reading a word.

Frank Zappa, the leader of the Mothers of Invention, a revolutionary rock group, believed the world could be turned topsy-turvy with wild strains from an electric guitar. He was right.

Frankie Avalon is one of several sweet Philadelphia boys who made it big with very little singing talent. He did manage to parlay his diminutive size into a "cuddle me" persona that Annette Funicello and the Mouseketeers found rather appealing. But *Beach Blanket Bingo* entertainment never did turn me on.

Gene Vincent, a rock artist, is included in my pantheon of fifties rock stars, even though I'm sure that he appears on no one else's list of former greats. The explanation is simple. When Vincent recorded "Be Bop a Lula," a marvelously rhythmic tune that let me "move out," he seemed to finish the song by building to a crescendo; but instead of scaling down, he cried out, "One more time." There was something inexplicably appealing about that. And even though its been done many times since then, I always think that someone's doing an imitation of Gene Vincent. More often than not, I'm right.

Greenberg's Brownies. I'm convinced that Greenberg's bakery was organized as a plot to get all of Manhattan's skinny people into "big men" shops. Once you've tasted their brownies, you know that you will go to any length to get them. When Mike Nichols was filming *Catch 22* in Mexico, he would have Greenberg's send him two dozen brownies each day. The lure of Greenberg's brownies is so great that I sometimes travel to New Jersey via Eighth Avenue to stock up on them.

Gucci's. Gucci is an Italian economist who came to the startling conclusion that the theory of supply and demand was wrong. He felt that by increasing price, you may be able to increase demand. To prove his hypothesis, he opened a Fifth Avenue store that sells scarves for forty dollars at such a fast rate that you might think they were being peddled from an Orchard Street pushcart. Everything sold bears the initial "G" or the name "Gucci," a device that may be the best advertising gimmick since the Goodyear blimp. Sales people in the store are generally so standoffish that a simple sale is usually a twenty-minute ordeal. Of course, you're paying for that time.

Horn & Hardart. When I was a kid, Horn & Hardart restaurants were the only place where I'd eat vegetables. So each week my folks took me there. The creamed spinach and baked beans were always sensational. In the last ten years the chain has been invaded by addicts, drunks, pimps, and prostitutes who sit there all night drinking a fifteen-cent cup of coffee. The chain has, as of late, attempted to revive business by featuring live music. But at a recent jam session which I attended, it seemed to me that the drunks and addicts were doing the playing.

I. F. Stone, alias Isidore Feinstein, is the last of the liberal heroes who can be described as having impeccable credentials. His *Bi-Weekly* had as great an influence on my attitudes as any speech of J.F.K.'s. Stone opposed American involvement in Vietnam before Pentagon planners had even located the place on their map of Asia. He anticipated the revisionist position on the Korean War while Noam Chomsky was still in diapers. His articles are probably the only required reading in *The New York Review* because he still manages to provide factual ammunition (admittedly selective facts) to counter government claims.

John Leonard is editor of the *New York Times Book Review*. He has tremendous influence over the fate of those books which have been reviewed in the Sunday paper and almost no influence on public reading tastes.

J.V. stands for junior varsity, a team designation which means that you are either too young or not good enough to play with the varsity. It may mean that you're in Coach's doghouse. It also means that no cheerleader in her right mind will go out with you.

Kangaroo, for New Yorkers, does not evoke an image of a marsupial from Down Under. It can either refer to a kid from the schoolyard who can jump thirty-two inches off the ground from a standing position or to a member of the Boys' High basketball team; both descriptions are clearly mutually compatible.

Knishes are a delightful Jewish delicacy which can be bought in most delicatessens—if you don't mind eating food that is two years old. Knishes come in many varieties, and all are guaranteed to give you heartburn. My favorite is "kasha," though my WASP friends prefer to call it buckwheat. Although knishes can be eaten in many New York restaurants, there are two knish establishments that sell little else. Yonah Schimmel's on the Lower East Side, a health inspector's nightmare, serves knishes to its patrons

164

via a dumbwaiter; if you keep your eyes closed, each morsel is a treat—but your eyes must remain closed. Mrs. Stahl's knish place at Brighton Beach Avenue has almost as many varieties of knishes as Howard Johnson's ice-cream flavors. The big seller this year is cabbage, a fact that Sam-behind-the-counter attributes to its low-calorie content.

Le Drugstore was a chic East Side meeting place where everything but drugs were sold (legally). It was *the* place to be on Friday nights, when plans for the weekend were being established. More often than not, its patrons never went inside, which partially explains why the establishment went out of business. They drove their Jaguars to the door and stared at the crowd seated outside. To combat the hazards of unruly crowds, the management put sharp metal spokes on the stoop. Mistaking the place for a zoo—which it was—the herd migrated down Third Avenue when Le Drugstore closed; they congregated at Daly's Dandelion, the nearest watering hole.

Leadbelly, a black convict from the South, was as much a regional voice of America as Joel Chandler Harris's Uncle Remus. Through his folk music, he made the rural South come alive. If you haven't heard the old record of his "Rock Island Line," you haven't heard American folk music.

Lindy's, a restaurant made famous by Damon Runyon, was located in the heart of the theatrical district. On any given night, one might walk by and see Ethel Barrymore, Bing Crosby, or Joe Louis seated at a table. More often than not, one could see me there, too. Being a cheesecake freak, I went there as often as I could. Since its closing, several years ago, I've continued my search for a cheesecake that can compare with the one I so vividly recall eating at Lindy's.

The Lion's Head, located near Sheridan Square, is a great place for draft beer, smoky air, and arguments about whether Mantle, Mays, or DiMaggio was the greatest modern center fielder. On any given evening, Pete Hamill, Norman Mailer, or the editorial staff of the *Village Voice* might be found at the bar, screaming that someone—perhaps the person they were sitting next to—was full-of-shit.

The Long Island Expressway, one of New York's many highways, has been called the longest parking lot in the world. It would be more accurately described as an automobile graveyard, since a trip from New York to Great Neck usually takes twelve months—or the average life span of an American car. Rather than bring the heap home, most drivers leave the car on the service road, where automobile parts vultures disassemble it in less time than it took to put it together.

Lord and Taylor's is a department store where the elegant set shop when they are slumming on lower Fifth Avenue. It is competition for Bloomingdale's, but its styles are somewhat less trendy and its prices are "tastefully" higher.

Lutèce is the only gourmet restaurant in the world where one can eat sumptuous bluefish in a charming garden and turn blue when calculating the check. For those who can afford to frequent New York's gourmet restaurants, this one ranks very high on the list. Of course, there are only about one hundred gourmets in the entire city.

MacDougal Street is an area made famous by Bob Dylan's lyrics. For residents of Greenwich Village, it is a honky-tonk region where, on any random summer evening, a sailor can be seen fighting with a local stoop sitter. Although it has numerous head shops, the street is best known for its sounds and smells. Horns blare, Italian words that sound like "mink" are shouted back and forth, hawkers advertise their wares, kids scream, and *felaffel*, sausage, and tomato sauce give the air a curiously acrid fragrance.

Mamma Leone's. For those who can recall it, the old Madison Square Garden was located on Forty-Ninth Street and Eighth Avenue, around the corner from Mamma Leone's. It was therefore no coincidence that every jock over six foot four made a pilgrimage to Mamma's with cage scouts from places like Miami and Dayton. Despite countless visits to the restaurant, I can't recall whether the food was any good. All I did was describe my jump shot from the key for an hour and a half; the waiter served one course after another and removed my uneaten pasta before I even had a chance to plunge my fork into the bowl.

Marble Loaf. For growing boys in their teens, there was only one way to prepare for sleep: devour a marble loaf and a container of milk. To counter the parental charge that you were gluttonous, the cake was eaten in savory one-inch slices, until nothing was left for any other member of the family.

Max Ascoli, the brilliant political correspondent, made *The Reporter* one of those "must read" journals to which I subscribed—but rarely read. During the sixties, Ascoli and his magazine became victims of the messianic peace-love-brotherhood movement that allegedly wanted to hear diverse points of view, but didn't want to know the reasons why Ascoli supported L.B.J.'s Vietnam policy.

Max Rafferty, former Superintendent of Public Instruction in California, acted as if any literature this side of Orphan Annie would be injurious to the impressionable minds of school-age children who, I might add, have been weaned on a steady diet of "X" rated movies and center fold-outs in *Playboy* magazine.

Max's Kansas City was, for a short time, *the* place to be seen in the downtown area. It was a good spot to pick up a date, and the food wasn't all that bad. People describing themselves as artists could always be found there, a fact that made me wonder when they found time to practice their art. In recent years the place has been overrun by fags and third-rate rock groups, both of whom look much like the former resident artists.

Maxwell's Plum. Have you ever eaten a gourmet meal in a bordello? Maxwell's Plum is truly a multisensory experience. You can stuff your tummy with magnificently prepared steak and simultaneously watch the mating rituals of those at the bar. If you don't get indigestion as a result of this experience, you should consult with your physician immediately.

Girls from such metropolises as Westerly, Rhode Island, flock to this bar hoping to meet some wealthy, hip, East Side male who knows Joe Namath. Of course, East Side males know this. They can be found searching at the bar for girls from Westerly who will put out. It often leads to a conjugal bond—of about two months' duration.

Mays is a department store haven for lower-middle-class New Yorkers who prefer to shop from a rack. It is truly the only place in the city where the sales help don't bother you—they don't help you either.

Mickey & Sylvia were a husband and wife recording team of the fifties. Mickey played the guitar while Sylvia played at being a sex goddess. Sylvia was excellent at her work. She had a breathy, incantatory way of saying "baby" that was sexier than all the writhing Tina Turner does on the stage.

Mighty Joe Young. In an effort to capitalize on the fame of King Kong, Hollywood producers made a film called *Mighty Joe Young*. This imitation had little grace and almost no pathos. It also did not have Fay Wray.

Mr. Natural, Robert Crumb's irreverent comic-strip character, attacks the Establishment, capitalism, war, sexual conventions, tradition, aggressiveness, and just about anything else that an uptight fifties product might embrace.

Neptune Avenue connects Sheepshead Bay and Coney Island. In my youth, people could always be found lining the street on a hot summer day, watching the parade of slow-moving trolleys. Although it is not really notable in any important way, Neptune Avenue is still the site of the best bagel factory in New York.

New York Post. For many people the *New York Post* is simply New York's only afternoon newspaper. But this is only part of the story. The *New York Post* is gospel at every city schoolyard. It is read like the Torah—from right to left—so that the sports pages will be thoroughly scoured before one turns to Earl Wilson and Leonard Lyons. It is then folded into four rectangular parts and tucked into the back pocket of one's jeans for handy reference—when resolving such major arguments as Kareem Abdul Jabbar's field goal percentage.

Norman Podhoretz, the editor of *Commentary*, is a self-proclaimed liberal who, in recent years, has preferred to hold conservative positions. His brave admission that he wanted to "make it" with the New York literati made him a target of vituperation for every radical from Cambridge to Berkeley. It also made me subscribe to *Commentary*. Podhoretz presumably has an enemy named Jason Epstein, one of the founders of *The New York Review of Books*. In actual fact, however, both men proclaim enmity toward one another in order to increase the circulation of their respective journals.

North Shore of Long Island is the place you can't get to when you take the Long Island Expressway.

Orchard Street is probably the largest flea market in the world. You can find everything from pickles in a barrel to down-filled quilts. And you can ask for what you want in Russian, Italian, Spanish, Yiddish, Hebrew, and even in English. That doesn't mean that you'll get it, but it doesn't hurt to ask. A friend of mine bargained for twenty minutes before buying two dozen nylon stockings for three dollars. Elated over this coup, she rushed home to try on a pair. Upon opening the box, she discovered that the stockings had no feet. Infuriated, she went back to the stand and demanded a refund. The same proprietor with whom she had previously bargained for twenty minutes—with no language barrier—said, "Me no speaky English." She screamed, "You can give me a refund in any language." But he turned away and mumbled something in an odd tongue. A guy standing nearby nudged her and said, "At times like this he can only speak Urdu."

Paul Stuart is a clothing store that is de rigueur for the man who dresses tastefully and likes to impress his woman.

The carpets are so soft and the salesmen so meticulous that the prospective customer gets the feeling that he's a slob as soon as he enters the store and buys everything in sight. This usually results in ten years of permanent indebtedness.

Interestingly, Paul Stuart is located on the same street as Brooks Brothers. My Madison Avenue friends tell me that when you graduate to high fashion Paul Stuart is where you go. Of course, it actually makes little difference since the bite out of your budget is likely to reduce you to rags in no time.

Pete Hamill, a columnist for the *New York Post*, can be considered a member of the Mailer-Breslin gang. He epitomizes, better than any of his writing colleagues, the confusion and inconsistency that simultaneously emanates from his devotion to "radical chic" and *machismo*. One day he may lament the frequentation of Washington Square Park by local bums and addicts. He may even advocate the arrest of some pervert who leers at the attractive breasts of a young mother in the playground. But when steps are taken to put a fence around the park to keep out undesirables, or a drunk is arrested for spitting at a passerby, Hamill angrily and hyperbolically denounces "the siege psychology in the city" and the blatant disregard for civil liberties.

Phoney Joannie, an Al Capp character, was created as a result of the author's biliousness toward the entire counter culture. He obviously chose the right symbol to attack: Joan Baez. But in so doing he inadvertently revealed as many of his warts as hers. All any sensible reader of "Li'l Abner" can say is, they deserve each other.

Radical Chic, a term coined by Tom Wolfe, applies to any Marxist who opens a head shop and charges rip-off prices so that he can maintain his co-op apartment on Fifth Avenue. Of course, the term doesn't have to be used quite so narrowly. I recently encountered a woman in Kismet, Fire Island (where "radical chic" types congregate), who wore 14-karat gold earrings, had her hair done at Elizabeth Arden's, walked a well-groomed poodle, wore only embroidered dungarees, and possessed a shirt which had the words "La Prensa Prison, Puerto Rico, 104973" printed on the front. When I inquired about the shirt, she replied, "Oh, it's authentic, you know; I bought it at Bloomingdale's for twenty-five dollars." All I could say was, "I know where you can get that shirt much cheaper."

St. Nicholas Avenue runs parallel to a hill that divides upper Manhattan into east and west. In all other respects it is New York's equivalent of a demilitarized zone.

Sale on the Bowery. A Bowery sale is the only real bargain left in New York. Shirts can be bought for a dime and trousers for a half-dollar. You also get a bonus with every purchase—free lice.

Sam "The Man" Taylor is *the* king of rock musicians. For five years during the late fifties his saxophone made every one of his rock tunes a hit. He was the Chuck Berry of the horn, yet, like a lot of people from that era, he is almost totally forgotten today. Every once in a while I wake up in the middle of the night, my legs ready to dance to one of his wild solos, and I ask, "Where are you, Sam?"

Screaming Jay Hawkins was perhaps the wildest rock performer of the fifties. His "conk" would be the envy of every black activist this side of Eldridge Cleaver. When

172

he sang "I'll Put a Spell on You," every pore in his body exuded sweat; that, along with his grunts and screams, created a display of energy the likes of which even James Brown can't duplicate.

Screw is a magazine for lascivious New Yorkers—is there any other kind?—that is read only in the bathroom. If you have a yearly subscription you are usually screwed, since the editorial offices are predictably closed by the D.A.'s office every two months.

Senior Campers are oversexed kids between the ages of fourteen and sixteen. Their reason for going to summer camp as seniors is to leave the watchful, or at least proximate, eye of their parents so that they can surreptitiously arrange a midnight rendezvous while their counselors are sleeping—or doing the same thing as their campers.

Soft Touch at Twenty-five Feet. Every once in a while someone appears in the schoolyard with a certain magic in his fingers. He can take a shot from above the key; the basketball may hit the front rim and then, like a guided missile, pass through it with uncanny consistency. He soon becomes known as the man with the "touch"; and his shooting hand wins the respect of a surgeon's fingers.

Stickball is a game played with the stolen handle of your mother's best mop. Perhaps the most customary procedure to follow is to draw a box on a schoolyard wall to establish a strike zone, and then use the stick to hit homers over the fence, triples against the fence, doubles which hit the fence on a bounce, and singles which go past the opposing pitcher. While the game is being played, the opposing pitcher announces the activities. "Leading off for the New York Mets is . . ." These announcements often lead to as much controversy as those balls which hit the outside corner of the strike zone. "Whaddya mean, Harrelson is leading off; he only bats eighth."

The Stillman Diet is a diet that combines two ounces of protein with ten gallons of water. The plan is guaranteed to work because the dieter spends so much time in the bathroom that he is too far removed from the delicacies behind the refrigerator door.

Stroll Parties. The "stroll" was a dance invented by the Diamonds and based upon a song of the same name. In order to do the dance, one would flap one's arms and do a modified Jackie Gleason "away we go" routine down a long corridor lined with clapping participants. My "stroll" parties usually occurred at a fraternity house. After going down the line with a partner I liked, we wouldn't return for any additional dances.

Stuffing a Basketball is a phrase which bears no relation whatsoever to turkeys or other animals. It is mostly used by basketball aficionados to describe someone who can dunk with a flair. For schoolyard buffs there is only one stuffer—"Dr J"—Julius Erving of the New York Nets. He takes off at the foul line like a big bird and delights in smashing the ball through the hoop.

Susan Sontag is a clever, radical social critic who, after visiting North Vietnam, returned to her New York apartment convinced that the world would be better off if America incinerated itself.

Theodore Roszak, author of *The Making of a Counter Culture*, became so engrossed in his subject that one can now describe him as a *made* counter-culture author. He has become, if his most recent work is any indication, the arch-advocate of adversary culture. But after reading *Where the Wasteland Ends*, I could only conclude that his work marked the starting point.

Three Sewers. Since New York kids, even upper-middle-class kids, play games in the streets, it should come as no surprise that sewer covers are used as an index of one's athletic prowess. To hit three sewers in a stickball game means that you're the first to be selected when sides are chosen. It probably also means that you lead the Fourth Street Boys in home runs.

Three-sewer hitters are very rare. But every generation of stickball players usually has two of them—one for each side. In recent years there has only been one four-sewer hitter in the city: Willie Mays.

Tom Rath, English professors will tell you, is the main character in *The Man in the Grey Flannel Suit*, the 1954 best-seller. In fact, he's my spiritual father. He is a man who is very conscious of security. When told that a great opportunity may await him if he is willing to take a chance, he will look at the freezer and say, "So, what if I don't eat filet mignon every night!"

Tom Wolfe is a journalist best known for *The Pump House Gang* and *Radical Chic and Mau-Mauing the Flak Catchers*. He is one of the few contemporary social critics who has been panned by both *The New York Review* and *The National Review*; as a consequence, he has become my model journalist.

Touchy-Feely Sessions. At a time when the Human Potential Movement and ubiquitous encounter groups are mushrooming, it is not surprising to find that many people truly believe that one can discover the millennium simply by holding someone's arm. I never did understand how one could become more human by letting it all hang out. If the touchy-feely session is designed to promote sexual titillation, it may make sense, but any other effect is purely serendipitous—at least that is what an inordinate number of its participants tell me while I hold their arms.

Union Turnpike is an avenue in Queens that divides Flushing and Jamaica. It was also where I stood on street corners waiting for my dates, and where gang wars between the Parsons' Boys and the Corona Dukes were arranged.

William V. Shannon, a *New York Times* columnist with conventionally liberal *New York Times* views, is conventionally conservative on such matters as education, family life, and child-rearing practices. It makes me wonder if *New York Times* columnists prescribe for the government the very things they are unwilling to do themselves.

Woodstock has been described as the most successful rock festival ever held (although it has gradually been pushed into second place by the P.R. men who covered the recent Watkins Glen bash). Woodstock was milked by all participants—the young who attended and were the envy of their peers; the entrepreneurs who saw green on the muddy pasture; and the reporters of *The New York Times* who wanted to be in on the action. Woodstock was, in fact, an event, although exactly what kind I found difficult to tell. It may have been a sex-and-drug orgy to some; it was definitely a mud-slinging affair reminiscent of childhood—

but it was *not* a rock concert. Of the 300,000 individuals who allegedly attended, perhaps two percent were actually able to hear the music, and only one percent were so mildly stoned that they even cared.